To Joan —
From a fellow seminarian
(CTS) and a friend who is
glad to have you here
at Kendal —
Affectimately
Fred

God, Evil, and Human Learning

God, Evil, and Human Learning

A Critique and Revision of the Free Will Defense in Theodicy

Fred Berthold Jr.

State University of New York Press

Published by
State University of New York Press, Albany

© 2004 State University of New York
All rights reserved

Printed in the United States of America

For information, address State University of New York Press,
90 State Street, Suite 700, Albany, NY 12207

Production by Michael Haggett
Marketing by Anne M. Valentine

Library of Congress Cataloging-in-Publication Data

Berthold, Fred, 1922–

God, evil, and, human learning : a critique and revision of the free will defense in
theodicy / Fred Berthold, Jr.
p.cm.
Includes bibliographical references and indexes.
ISBN 0-7914-6041-X (alk. paper)—ISBN 0-7914-6042-8 (pbk. : alk. paper)
1. Free will and determination—Religious aspects—Christianity. 2. Theodicy.
3. Good and evil—Religious aspects—Christianity. I. Title.
BT810.3.B47 2004
233'.7–dc22   2004045244

10 9 8 7 6 5 4 3 2 1

This work is dedicated to my wife, Laura, with thanks for many years of love, understanding, and support.

Contents

"Then God said, 'Let us make man in our image and likeness'…"

(Genesis 1:26)

The task and joy of life lies in learning to become what we are meant to be.

Chapter 1

Introduction

Is it possible for a person who has a proper regard for his or her rational faculties, and for the evidence afforded by experience, to believe in the God who is the object of worship by Christians?

In this world there is so much suspicion, hatred, and cruelty, and so much grievous suffering, that is impossible for anyone with even a modest degree of open-mindedness to avoid questions or doubts about this God. Is this God, if indeed there be such a God, perhaps indifferent to the sufferings of humans? Yet Christians affirm that God is perfectly loving, that he gave his own son to make it possible for humans to overcome suffering. Is this God, if indeed there be such a God, perhaps too weak to defeat and banish the powers of evil? Yet Christians affirm that their God is omnipotent and that, by his divine providence, he is the ruler of the world.

Without doubt the so-called problem of evil constitutes the greatest intellectual obstacle to the Christian faith, or indeed any form of theistic belief. Though this problem has most often been discussed in connection with Christian theology, as I shall do, it was formulated before the Christian era, and it has a wider application. It is a central theme of the biblical book, Job. Perhaps the earliest precise formulation was given by Epicurus (342–270 B.C.), who wrote:

> God either wishes to take away evils, and is unable; or He is able and is unwilling; or He is neither willing nor able; or He is both willing and able. If He is willing and is unable, He is feeble, which is not in accordance with the character of God; if He is able and unwilling, He is envious,

1

which is equally at variance with God; if He is neither willing nor able,
He is both envious and feeble, and therefore not God; if He is both willing and able, which is alone suitable to God, from what source then are
evils? Or why does He not remove them?[1]

Within the Western theological tradition the effort to provide a solution to this problem has in modern times been called theodicy, adopting
the terminology of the philosopher Leibniz.[2]

In this work I want to focus on the free will defense. The free will
defense argues that God is responsible for none of the evils in the world,
but that they are rather due to the misuse of free will by humans (or initially
by the rebel angels and then by humans). According to the traditional
argument, God has a great goal for all humans: namely, the Kingdom of
God. The Kingdom of God is so infinitely good that it outweighs any and
all evils which may be unavoidable in the process of its attainment. The
Kingdom of God is a society in which humans freely love God and one
another. This goal requires that humans be created with free will, for no
relationship can be a genuinely loving one unless the love is freely given.
Having granted free will to humans, even God logically cannot prevent
them from choosing evil; and it is the misuse of free will that is the origin
of all evils. In its original state, as created by God, the world contained no
evil at all. All evil is either sin (misuse of free will) or the consequence of sin.

It has been widely held by Christian theologians that this defense provides us with an adequate theodicy. Moreover, none of the other arguments
or defenses, which have been developed, come anywhere close to cogency,
certainly not on their own and not unless included as an aspect of a free
will defense. Since my purpose is to see if the free will defense can be formulated in a maximally cogent way, I shall not dwell at length on other
arguments. The so-called contrast theory will later be discussed in some
detail because, though it cannot stand alone, it constitutes an important
element in the traditional free will defense, and also in the revised free will
defense which I shall develop. The eschatological argument clearly does
not belong in a theodicy; for theodicy seeks to offer rational arguments
and evidences to show that belief in the Christian God is compatible with
the fact that the world contains so many evils. The eschatological argument is not really an argument at all; it is an appeal to what, according
to the traditional Christian faith, the believer will experience and come
to know in the world to come after death. According to this belief, we
will then understand how the evils suffered in this world are overcome,
compensated for, and justified in the great cosmic plan of God.

In evaluating the traditional Christian free will defense, I shall focus on the formulation developed by Aurelius Augustine (354–430 A.D.). Not only was Augustine the first to develop this argument in its connection with the broadest possible treatment of Christian theological views, but his formulation has dominated subsequent traditional Christian theodicies in western Christendom.[3]

Though I note some serious difficulties with the Augustinian free will defense, I maintain it includes a very important, central, and valid insight, but an insight which could be rendered even more compelling. Indeed, the insight is embedded in a network of views and arguments many of which seem quite dubious or even on occasion offensive. However, to state this important insight baldly and briefly, it is the understanding that some of the greatest goods (including those essential to the Kingdom of God) could not exist except in contrast to, and indeed in struggle with, opposing evils. The cogency of the insight to which I refer depends, as we shall see, upon a certain basic value judgment which, though in my view reasonable, is yet debatable.

There are two judgments that are essential to the credibility of my own thesis: (1) the Augustinian insight to which I refer may properly be regarded as valid, and (2) the revision of the free will defense, which I shall develop strengthens the claim that it is valid. The Augustinian argument also has the virtue of indicating that there is a necessary connection between God's goodness and the evils of the world. My revised argument goes one step further and shows why there is and must be such a necessary connection. The necessity of this connection depends, in the version I develop, not merely on theological views, which unfortunately for any theodicy, rest upon revelation rather than evidence and reason; rather, the connection depends on logical implications of the very concept of free will.

By way of introduction I should also like to indicate some of the context for my thinking about evil and the free will defense. This may help the reader to understand where I'm coming from.

Both by education and by inclination I find congenial what might be called a rational-empirical approach to theology. It seems to me that humans have been created with rational capacities and that the Creator intended us to use them. I cannot agree with those who regard theodicy—the effort to give a rational answer to the question as to how there can be so much evil in a world created by God—as blasphemous.[4] The demand for the suppression of independent thought and reasoning is not consistent with the concept, certainly implied in Christian theology, that the goal God has in mind for humans is that they come to offer, with a free will, their love to God, and to one another. As we shall see, acquiring the abilities that constitute free will depends, among other things, upon the development of our rational control of our desires and volitions (see chapter 6). The empirical aspect of my orientation has to do with the conviction that, for human beings, any religious experience or concept acquires meaning for us only to the extent that it chimes in with, and is illuminated by, our other human experiences. For example, the notion that God is love would be unintelligible to us unless we had some ordinary human experience of love.

By education and conviction I accept as valid the modern historical-critical study and interpretation of the Bible, and indeed of all religious texts. This is implied by the comments and illustrations in chapter 4.

I have been impressed and influenced by so-called feminist theology. For one thing, the traditional application of male gender to God reflects a time and culture-bound bias, as well as an anthropomorphic view. Moreover, that bias has generally been coupled in the tradition with a view of God as a completely domineering, and indeed rather tyrannical, power. For my further criticism of this traditional bias, see the section headed, New Perspectives, in chapter 8.

My rejection of the anthropomorphic and male gender bias mentioned above has also been influenced by one aspect of what is called postmodernist thought. This aspect has sometimes been given the awesome label of nonfoundationalism.[5] The gist of this view is that no human claims to final and indisputable knowledge of any sort of reality are valid. There are no bedrock foundations of certainty with regard to any such knowledge claims. It is, no doubt, the aspiration of humans to attain such knowledge, and it is the feeling of many modern folk that such knowledge is attained in some of the basic natural sciences. But such aspirations are never fully and completely fulfilled. Quite a long time ago, Immanuel Kant made it clear that such limitations apply to all claims to know the truth about anything that transcends the spatio-temporal world, which is our natural human environment. (See footnote number 34 on page 99).

This nonfoundationalism chimes in well with another modern movement that has influenced me: namely, logical positivism or logical empiricism. After a considerable flirtation with that way of thought, I came away with the conviction that they had made at least one positive contribution: namely, a clarification of what is implied in any claim to knowledge in any rational, scientific sense. This has led me to a view regarding the relationship between knowledge and faith—a view which still seems valid to me. We do not know God; our specifically theological beliefs do not constitute knowledge. This is to concede that the term knowledge in our modern culture has come to mean statements with regard to observable states of affairs, which are in principle replicable and verifiable in a public way by other humans without regard to special cultural or religious background.[6]

To concede this is by no means to deny that faith plays a very important and valid role in our lives and beliefs. But belief is not knowledge in the sense described above; nor is faith. The statements of faith go beyond what is in principle verifiable in the sense given above. But the statements of faith, which I shall offer in a number of places in this work, and especially in chapter 7, and also in the rather speculative chapter 8, must, in order to be valid in my own view, be logically coherent and consistent with our ordinary knowledge. We do not know God, but we have intimations, feelings, and experiences, which come to human beings quite universally in visions and myths, dramatic, poetic, and prophetic utterances, and writings. These things are by no means to be despised as a lower or less important aspect of our thoughts; for it is through such revelations that we discover purpose, guidance, and value for our lives.

So much, then, for the context of my thinking. Whether it bears worthy fruit must be judged by the reader in view of what follows.

Chapter 2

The Central Importance of the
Free Will Defense

The so-called free will defense is of central importance to any theodicy because the other main arguments, which have been put forward, are quite weak in themselves: that is, unless they are made an integral component within the free will defense.

No Christian theodicy denies the reality of many evils in the world.[1] Acknowledging these evils, the most general strategy of Christian theodicy has been to try to show that God permits these evils because it is logically impossible for him to achieve his great goal, the Kingdom of God, without granting free will to humans; and, having granted them free will, it is logically impossible for Him to prevent them from doing what is in itself evil and also productive of further evils.

Apart from the free will defense, the two other main arguments that have been put forward do not even come close to showing that there is a necessary connection between God's great goal and the evils of the world. If one cannot show there is such a necessary connection, then the evils of the world are gratuitous. By a gratuitous evil I mean one that is either not necessary or that is avoidable, in connection with God's attainment of his great goal. If God permits, or causes, a single evil that is gratuitous, it would seem to follow that He is, just to that extent, less than perfectly good, and, therefore, not the God proclaimed by the Christian faith.

As we shall see, it is not clear that even the traditional free will defense is able to show that there are no gratuitous evils. But it does purport to do this, and it has seemed to many that it has succeeded in doing so.

THE TRADITIONAL FREE WILL DEFENSE

In the most general sense the free will defense involves the claim that the evils of the world are not due to a defect in God's creation, or a lack of benevolence on his part, but rather to the misuse of free will on the part of his creatures. There have been many variations on this theme by many writers. In order to describe and assess what I call the traditional free will defense, without producing a long historical treatise, I propose to focus on the version articulated by one theologian, Aurelius Augustine. This, I contend, is much less arbitrary than it might seem, because Augustine's thought dominated the western tradition to an extraordinary degree. I shall give a summary of his views in my own words, supplemented by a number of quotes from his works.

A SUMMARY OF AUGUSTINE'S THEODICY

God is the sole creator of the world, which is an expression of his abundant and overflowing love. Since God is perfect in goodness, wisdom, and power, the world He creates is perfect. The perfection of the world is not, however, identical with God's own perfection, for that would be, *per impossibile*, to create a second God. The created world is made up of many things in a harmonious order of graded perfections, each thing exhibiting its peculiar good and contributing to a totality, which as a whole is perfect. Each created thing also differs from God in a crucial respect, His goodness is immutable, whereas the goodness of all created beings is mutable. Among the most excellent of created beings are angels and humans, and their excellence consists especially in their rational capacities and their free will. Free will is essential so that their virtues may properly be called their own, and so that they may freely choose to love God and one another. The latter is genuine only if chosen by free will. The choice of love is the greatest good for these created beings, for it is in loving that they attain the image of God in and for which they were created[2] and also because love, along with justice, is the chief constituent of God's great goal, the Kingdom of God. The Kingdom of God is a society of rational beings who freely love God and one another and who live together in justice. But since these creatures are mutable, it is possible for them to turn their love not to God but to lesser things, or to themselves. There is nothing in the created world that is essentially evil; yet turning towards a lesser good on the part of a rational creature constitutes an evil will. When this is done, the perfect harmony of creation is disrupted and corrupted. For some reason[3] some of the angels turned away from God, and this was the first origin of evil in the world.

> The cause of evil is the defection of the will of a being who is mutably good from the Good that is immutable. This happened first in the case of the angels and, afterwards, that of man.[4]

This sin, turning away from God, first by Satan and then by Adam and Eve, is the source of all evil in the world. For this sin, as we shall see, is the root of all subsequent sin. "All that we call evil is either sin or the punishment for sin."[5]

Clearly, we need an explanation of why an omnipotent and perfectly good God would create a world with the potentiality for such great evil, all the while foreseeing that these evils would in fact be realized. Augustine's theodicy was so influential in part because he was the first major theologian to provide an answer to this question in the context of an absolutely all-embracing world history in which God's great plan for the world constitutes the leit motif.

When we see the total picture, we understand, so Augustine believed, that the creation of beings with free will, even though aware they would misuse their free will and cause the rise of such great evils, is not only justified but is an expression of the perfect benevolence of God. For God's great goal is the realization of the Kingdom of God, a good so great that it more than compensates for all evil; and, given that goal, the creation of angels and humans with free will was necessary.

Having created beings with free will, God permits evil; for, having created beings with a will that is free, God can not logically prevent them from choosing what is evil. Of course, God, being Himself free and omnipotent, and already perfect, without any addition of a created world, and foreseeing the evils which would arise in the world he planned, could have refrained from creating any world at all. Then there would have been no evil at all. Why, given the grievous evils he knew would arise, did not God refrain from creating this world?

Under these conditions, does not His creation indicate some lack of goodness on God's part? No! For God also planned and foreknew that out of all this evil an even greater good would arise.

> By his omniscience, God could foresee two future realities: how bad man whom God had created good was to become, and how much good God was to make out of this very evil.[6]

> For God never would have created any, I do not say angel, but even man, whose future wickedness he foreknew, unless he had equally known to what uses in behalf of the good he could turn them, thus embellishing the course of the ages, as it were an exquisite poem set off with antitheses.[7]

The greater good is manifest in two ways: through the grace by which he redeems those whom he has elected to save; and by the justice he exhibits in punishing those who remain in sin.

According to Augustine, the eternal punishment of the reprobate contributes not only to the psychological bliss of the redeemed but to the ontological perfection of the universe!

> Since there is happiness for those who do not sin, the universe is perfect; and it is no less perfect because there is misery for sinners. ... The penalty of sin corrects the dishonor of sin.[8]

I turn now to a consideration of the other two main arguments that have characterized traditional Christian theodicies: the argument which depends upon the contrast theory, and an eschatological argument.

THE CONTRAST THEORY

In some of Augustine's works, the so-called contrast theory is articulated as an independent argument, even though it is implicit in his free will defense. After having developed the concept of free will, I shall indicate how and why elements of the contrast theory are necessary parts of an adequate free will defense.

The contrast theory argues that in order for God to attain his great goal it was necessary for him to create a world in which contrasts between good and evil would arise. What sort of contrast is implied?

Let us quickly set aside as unacceptable (in any Christian context) the notion that there can be no good without contrasting evils. The language used by some writers might seem to suggest this.[9] However, Christian tradition has insisted that even before anything else existed, God alone existed and that he was and is perfectly good.

Sometimes the contrast theory is articulated with reference to states of human awareness or appreciation. The general notion is that we would not be aware of the good or appreciate it if there were no contrasting evils. For example, if there were no dangers of any kind, we would not be aware of any actions as being courageous, nor would we have any reason for developing a concept of courage. If there were no instances of poverty or hunger we would not think of any actions as being generous.

I have two objections to this line of reasoning. First, this sort of contrast does not support the argument that God, in order to attain his great goal, had to create a world with contrasting goods and evils. If the world were such that we never had any reason to formulate a concept of courage, for example, this would seem to indicate how perfectly good such a world would be! Second, it is simply not the case that humans could not be aware of and appreciate the most important virtues, from a Christian standpoint, in the absence of contrasting evils. Perhaps there is, somewhere, a person who has only had contact with other persons who are always generous and loving. Such a person would, I suggest, be fully conscious of generosity and love, and fully appreciative of it, even if he or she had never formulated the concepts of generosity or love. If in fact there is no such person, there is no reason why the omnipotent God might not have made such to exist, or indeed to be the universal situation for humans.

God could have made humans so that everyone would be musicians and all enormously enjoy fine music. Some might be able to produce or perform only mediocre music, while others might have the genius of a Mozart or a Yo Yo Ma. The music of the latter would bring exquisite joy even in the absence of very poor and annoying counterexamples.

It is probably true that in the world as it is, and with humans constituted as they are, we appreciate good more keenly after experiencing contrasting evil. But in the context of mainline Christian tradition, this argument lacks cogency because there is no good reason why an omnipotent God should not have constituted the world and humans differently.

There is, however, another form of the contrast theory, which is more convincing: namely, in terms of the Christian perspective, some of the very highest goods are essentially and necessarily linked to opposing evils. In the interest of brevity I shall articulate this point with reference to only one such highest good. Over and over again, Christian thinkers have insisted that love is the highest good.[10] Indeed, love is regarded as the most essential attribute of God's own being and nature; and it is the power that motivated the creation of the word; and it is the supreme virtue which is to adorn the Kingdom of God. Clearly, too, from the Christian perspective, the very highest form and expression of love is the forgiving love of Jesus Christ.

But there could be no forgiving love if there were nothing to forgive. Love is at its greatest, according to this view, when at great cost it reaches out to those who are living in sin, alienated from God. It should come as no surprise that Christians have thought in terms of this contrast, for they have held that the most complete and perfect revelation of God's nature and will is to be found in Jesus the Christ, and most strikingly in his sacrificial death to redeem sinners. This contrast is celebrated in a striking passage in the Roman Catholic mass for the evening before Easter, in words frequently, but questionably, attributed to Augustine: "O most happy fault [or sin], which made possible and necessary such and so great a redeemer."[11]

We must concede that this claim is valid within the context of a Christian theology framed to reconcile faith in God with the evils in the world as it actually is. From the Christian point of view, this claim is valid in its contention that the very highest good could not exist in this world in the absence of opposing evil. But does this version of the contrast theory do the job for theodicy which has been claimed for it?

We might note that this argument, even if valid, does not help meet the challenge presented by natural evils. But, apart from that, two objections occur to me: (1) the cost is too great, especially since (2) the same great good could be achieved in a world which includes things that need to be forgiven, but in a world in which these are fewer and less grievous than those which obtain in the actual world.

1.   The cost is too great. There is, according to the Christian faith, to be an eventual triumph of good over evil. There is to be the experience of and joyful appreciation of the peace, justice, and love of the Kingdom of God. Here, we must remind ourselves that most of the traditional theologians, like Augustine, thought that the vast majority of humankind would experience not this bliss but rather unspeakable suffering. *When we consider the vast extent and enormity of the evils which exist in this actual world, it is reasonable to ask whether the eventual victory for an exclusive few is worth the cost.*

     The plausibility of the traditional free will defense clearly depends, among other things, upon certain basic value judgments. The claim is made that God has permitted (or caused) evil to exist in order that from it he might bring about a greater good. Is that good good enough to compensate for all of the evils of our actual world? I shall discuss the nature of basic value judgments, and what is required to justify them (in chapter 7), where I shall present my revised free will defense.

2.   *The great goal could be achieved in a world which contains fewer and less grievous evils. It seems to me that, if we retain the traditional concept of divine omnipotence, this conclusion is inevitable.*

After developing a more adequate concept of free will than generally found in the tradition, as in chapter 6, we will see that some natural and moral evils are necessary if humans are to be able to learn the capacities of free will. Of course, some are necessary in the *O Felix Culpa* scheme of things, but, given divine omnipotence, I see no reason why there need be so many and such horrible evils as exist in our world. I see nothing illogical in the notion that the world and humanity might have been constituted by an omnipotent God in such a way that there were some evils in the world, but of a milder sort, and that humans might have been so made as to be much more inclined to learn from their experience of those evils to become far more helpful and loving towards one another than humans in fact are in our world.

If God is omnipotent, as that has been understood traditionally, he could have arranged a world in which there are indeed actual evils, but not so many of them and not such virulent ones. Actual evils are necessary, according to the view now under discussion, so that persons might themselves freely learn to choose what is right and so that they would come to understand and appreciate the virtues of the Kingdom of God. But surely one could learn to distinguish between good and evil, and to appreciate the good, through some rather limited number of experiences. Even if the number were rather large, it would be better than the situation in our actual world, where the evils seem never to end, but perhaps even to multiply. In any case, the evils of the world seem to be out of control. And that is the point: God could, if omnipotent, keep evils under control yet permit sufficient evil for persons to learn to freely embrace the good—yes, even to learn through struggle and suffering, but not to such an extent as in the actual world.

There is a significant strand in the Christian tradition that suggests a possible way to reply to my objections. It has to do with a basic value judgment, which is implicit in much that Christians are won't to say about the evils of this world. What I think of as a super heroic version of the Christian life would look with scorn upon what I have suggested. A puny, untested, and weak kind of life, they would conclude, wholly unworthy of those who are supposed to be disciples of Christ, whose struggle and sacrifice overcame the power of Satan. No! To become worthy of citizenship in the Kingdom of God, a saint must endure the greatest battles imaginable against the powers of evil, that his or her virtues may be tested and tempered.

The Christian New Testament often pictures the struggles of Jesus Christ, and his disciples along the lines of a great literary tragedy. The ultimate victory of the hero is incomparably great because he battles with and overcomes the greatest powers of evil. Thus, Christ must win the victory not only over his human opponents but also against those principalities and powers against which his disciples must now contend (i.e. "against the principalities, against the powers, against the world rulers of this present darkness, against the spiritual hosts of wickedness in the heavenly places"). Against these evils we must "take the whole armor of God, that you may be able to stand in the evil day, and having done all, to stand."[12]

One might take the line that the true and proper greatness of the great goal is attainable only through a terrible and costly struggle against evil, one in which the hero (saint) must endure the greatest suffering possible, suffering not confined by divine fiat and overcome only by the valor of the hero. This is to push the contrast theory to its highest pitch.

In the great classical tragedies and even in the most banal modern TV thriller, the victory of the good guy(s) over the forces of evil is enhanced, when the bad guy(s) are portrayed in the most demonic and evil manner possible.

Is it legitimate to transfer this sort of aesthetic judgment to the realm of moral values? Or, indeed, does not the value of the aesthetic victory over evil derive from our basic moral value judgments?

It seems to me to strain our credulity to a considerable degree, but not to be downright irrational, to argue that the incomparable nature of the good which the Christian faith celebrates can be attained only by victory over incomparable evils, and, moreover, that we humans can appreciate the greatness of the value only when we see it in the context of that great struggle. Nevertheless, this whole line of defense is rendered dubious, in my view, by the enormous amount and virulence of the evils of this world, and by the fact that so relatively few experience the victory and so many experience only defeat and misery.

Clearly this super heroic view depends, as I have said, upon a basic value judgment. That such judgments are not clearly demonstrable by reason as correct, or as incorrect, is discussed in chapter 7.

AN ESCHATOLOGICAL ARGUMENT

Another argument often put forward might be called the eschatological argument. This argument is usually tacked on to the free will defense. It goes like this. God permits evils in this world, because his great goal, the Kingdom of God, requires that humans have free will; and, having granted free will, God necessarily also allows its misuse, otherwise the will would not be truly free; and it is from this misuse of free will that evils arise. But ultimately all of the evils of this world will be more than balanced by an incommensurable good, for in the Kingdom of God all persons will freely love one another and God, and will live in perfect justice, enjoying moreover the joy of the presence of God.

We may note in passing that this argument seems to assume that the contrast theory, as presented above, is inadequate or weak. It assumes, namely, that without some radical correction in the world to come, the balance of good and evil, as we know it in this world, seems to count against the goodness and justice of God.

Clearly this eschatological argument has no place in a rational theodicy, which seeks to justify the ways of God to man through arguments based upon reason and evidence. It is, indeed, at home in a fideist context, with those who argue that a rational theodicy is presumptuous and that we must rely upon faith alone. For the belief that there will be a more than compensating good in the Kingdom of God is clearly based upon faith, which in turn rests upon the authority of the Bible.

Even if we accept the notion that there will be such a glorious ultimate outcome, we must ask whether the great sufferings of so many in this world are necessary. As noted earlier (see p. 7), it is not sufficient to show that evils are more than compensated for by greater goods; one must also show that there are no gratuitous evils. The eschatological argument, even when supplemented by the traditional free will defense, does not provide an adequate answer to this problem.

So, given the focus of this work, I should perhaps give this argument extremely short shrift. The eschatological argument, however, especially in the way in which it has been often elaborated in the tradition, gives rise to several grave difficulties for those who are trying to work out a rational theodicy.

One difficulty arises for all traditional free will defenders: namely, if God will ultimately bring about a good so great as to compensate for all of the evils of the world, why does he not arrange for all to participate in this good? The traditional answer is that this would not be just for there are those who deserve to be punished by the torments of hell. It is necessary here to note that there are two variations of the traditional answer: one is found in what I identify (for simplicity) as the augustinian/calvinistic variation and the other as the thomistic variation. Neither variant is convincing.

It would seem that God, if wholly loving and good, would save from damnation all he could save. Given the augustinian and calvinistic systems, it would seem he certainly could save all. All are born in sin and naturally so corrupted that they deserve the punishment of hell. God gratuitously redeems some by his unmerited grace. Since there is no condition in the sinner that is a necessary condition for election to salvation by God, and since it is wholly arbitrary so far as any deserving is concerned, why could not (and would not) a loving God extend this saving grace to all? There is no good answer to this question in the system under discussion. Such theologians say it is blasphemous to pry into the judgments of God, but this of course is just another expression of the fideist attack upon all theodicy. It is also sometimes said (without benefit of prying?) that God allows some to be condemned in order to add to the total perfection of the universe (see p. 10 above for Augustine's statement on this). That this would add to the perfection of the universe seems not only doubtful but perverse!

If one takes the thomistic stance, there seems to be a somewhat more reasonable solution to the problem under discussion. All are not saved, because some are not worthy. Some are justly condemned because their sins are a result of their own freely chosen evil actions. We are not just born into total depravity, as with the other line of thought. We have sufficient power of free will to choose the good. True, we need the aid of divine grace, but it is freely offered to all, and we can choose to accept it. So, if we remain in sin, it is our own fault, and we are worthy of damnation. The problem with this is that given the thomistic and the generally traditional notion of God's omnipotence, there is no reason why God could not and should not have constituted human beings to be less prone to choose what is evil; or that he should not pour out his redeeming grace upon all in such abundance as to persuade all to freely accept it.

The traditional notion that humans are born totally depraved (Augustine/Calvin) or so morally weakened that they often choose what is wrong (Aquinas), holds that this moral depravity, or weakness, is a consequence of the sin of Adam (and Eve). The ideas that (1) Adam and Eve committed a sin so heinous as to deserve all of the punishment brought upon them and their descendents, and (2) that all subsequent humans inherit the depravity and therefore justly deserve the punishment—these ideas are essential to the free will defense as developed in western Christianity. The notion that Adam and Eve committed a crime worthy of such dire punishment cannot be sustained. For full culpability presumes free will, and, as depicted in the tradition, they lacked the conditions necessary for the development of free will (see p. 17).

Moreover, the notion that their sin and punishment can properly be inherited by subsequent humans cannot be sustained. Here I summarize the cogent critique articulated by Soren Kierkegaard. The traditional view of Adam, says Kierkegaard, places him "fantastically outside the human race."[13] He is the only one who does not become a sinner by inheriting the original sin. He begins his life in innocence and makes the transition to sinfulness by his own free choice. Subsequent humans, on the other hand, begin their lives as sinners and unlike Adam, they possess no free will unless and until redeemed by the grace of God in Christ. In view of the enormous importance given to sin and to free will, it is doubtful that prelapsarian Adam and postlapsarian humans are of the same species. This indicates that the notion of the solidarity of the human race, as determined by Adam, is seriously flawed. The notion that humans subsequent to Adam properly inherit his sin is also without warrant.

> Consequently, every attempt to explain Adam's significance for the race as *caput generis humani naturale, seminale, foedrale* (head of the human race by nature, by generation and by covenant), to recall the expression of dogmatics, confuses everything. He is not essentially different from the race, for in that case there is no race at all; he *is* not the race, for in that case also there would be no race.[14]

The concept of free will developed in chapter 6 should also make it clear that free will is not some sort of faculty that can just be given to a person, even by God. It is rather a complex set of abilities, which are learned as one's rational capacities mature and in the context of experience in dealing with various actual goods and evils, and their consequences. One's free will is not truly free unless it is autonomous; and if it is not, then one cannot be held responsible, certainly not fully responsible so as to warrant the dire consequences meted out to Adam and Eve and all their progeny.

Kierkegaard also points out that the traditional description of Adam not only places him fantastically outside the human race, but also implies that Adam was innocent in such a way that he could not be held fully responsible for his actions.

> When it is stated in *Genesis* that God said to Adam, "Only from the tree of the knowledge of good and evil you must not eat," it follows as a matter of course that Adam has not understood this word, for how could he understand the difference between good and evil when this distinction would follow as a consequence of the enjoyment of the fruit?[15]

In summary: the other two main arguments, other than the free will defense, which have been put forward in traditional theodicies, suffer serious flaws. The contrast theory cannot stand on its own but makes a contribution when properly included in an adequate formulation of the free will defense. The eschatological argument does not properly belong in a theodicy at all, and moreover, in its traditional form, raises insurmountable problems.

Therefore, it is all the more unfortunate, that the free will defense in its traditional form also has serious flaws. The most serious of these flaws arise from the fact that the theologians who developed it worked with an inadequate concept of free will itself. In chapter 6, I develop a more adequate concept of free will and indicate how, in its light, the traditional free will defense is unacceptable. Then I move on to a reformulation of the free will defense (chapter 7). In chapter 3, I discuss another line of criticism that must be faced both by the traditional free will defense and by the version I shall ultimately propose. I want to deal with this criticism at this point because I regard this criticism as the most devastating argument that can be brought against the traditional free will defense.

Chapter 3

Why Doesn't God Cause Us to Have a Wholly Virtuous Free Will?

According to the traditional free will defense, it was essential (given his goal) that God create humans with free will. This is because his goal, the Kingdom of God, is a society in which humans freely love God and one another. On the other hand, the traditional argument, at least in the influential form developed by Augustine, traces all evil in the world to the misuse of free will. Why did not God give humans free will and at the same time arrange that they never misuse it?

In view of traditional doctrines of divine providence and omnipotence, it would seem that God could have arranged this. Surely God, being omnipotent, could (and according to some theologians, like Calvin, did) cause all things to happen precisely as determined by his will. And, if there is no logical contradiction involved in having a will that is free and at the same time determined, then God could have caused all humans to have wholly virtuous free wills.

The traditional doctrine of divine providence asserts that all things are governed by the eternal plan and explicit will of God. The traditional doctrine of divine omnipotence holds that God can do anything whatsoever that is conceivable without logical contradiction. The free will defense assigns responsibility for sin (and the introduction of evil into the world) to the misuse of free will by humans (and some like Augustine would add by angels even before the fall of humans). As to the relation between personal moral responsibility and free will the testimony of the tradition is, alas, rather confused and unclear. Most have held that persons can be held morally responsible only if they act with free will, and I believe it is the case that all have held that this was true of Adam before the Fall. But Calvin (and Luther and perhaps Augustine) held that unredeemed persons after the Fall do not possess free will and are yet morally responsible for their actions.

The discussion of these issues, among other things, makes it clear that one of the greatest obstacles to developing an adequate free will defense is the fact there is no consensus within the tradition regarding the proper concept of free will. Indeed, none of the great and influential theologians developed the concept of free will in the detail and with the adequacy that is needed. We cannot decide whether there is or is not a logical contradiction in saying that some human actions are done with free will and are completely determined in such a way that the agent is also morally responsible for her or his action, unless we are clear as to the meaning of the term free will.

THE CHALLENGE OF MACKIE AND FLEW

Let us return to the question of this chapter: why doesn't God cause humans to have a wholly virtuous free will? This is the challenging question put to the Christian theologian by two contemporary philosophers.[1] According to Professors John L. Mackie and Antony Flew, the traditional free will defense is invalid because God could have arranged for (caused) a world in which humans have free will and in which they are so constituted by God that they would always freely choose the good. If this is so, then God could have attained his great goal, the Kingdom of God in which persons freely love God and one another, without the evils which plague our actual world.[2] That he has not done so indicates that he lacks either the power or the benevolence to do so, or it indicates that no such being exists.

Mackie adopts certain premises:

> Good is opposed to evil in such a way that a good thing always elimi-
> nates evil as far as it can, and ... there are no limits to what an omnipo-
> tent thing can do. From these it follows that a good omnipotent thing
> eliminates evil completely, and then the propositions that a good
> omnipotent thing exists, and that evil exists, are incompatible.[3]

I cite this passage, which perhaps puts things in an overly simple way, to indicate that his attack upon the free will defense occurs within the context of an attack upon Christian theism generally. He holds that it is possible to show not only "that religious beliefs lack rational support, but that they are positively irrational, that the several parts of the essential theological doctrine are inconsistent with one another. ..."[4] Mackie's argument against the free will defense is as follows:

> If God has made men such that in their free choices they sometimes prefer what is good and sometimes what is evil, why could he not have made men such that they would always freely choose the good? If there is no logical impossibility in a man's choosing the good on one, or on several occasions, there cannot be a logical impossibility in his freely choosing the good on every occasion. God was not, then, faced with a choice between making innocent automata and making beings who, in acting freely, would sometimes go wrong. There was open to him the obviously better possibility of making beings who act freely but always go right. Clearly his failure to avail himself of this possibility is inconsistent with his being both omnipotent and wholly good.[5]

Both Mackie and Flew argue that acts of free will are not uncaused, but are rather caused by the character of the agent, and the omnipotent God could arrange for the character to be formed in such a way that it would be wholly virtuous (i.e., would always freely choose the good). In this argument Mackie and Flew are clearly exemplifying the compatibilist doctrine, which holds that there is no contradiction between an action's being an act of free will and its being completely determined.

Flew says that he is launching a skeptical counterattack upon the key claim of the free will defense: "the idea that there is a contradiction involved in saying that God might have made people so that they always freely choose the right."[6] He describes a paradigm case of acting freely: two young people choosing to get married where there is no problem of having to get married, no parental or other undue pressure, or the like. The two decide to get married because they want to. They are of an age to know their own minds, and there were alternatives which each had considered and had been perfectly free to choose. But, says Flew, speaking in what follows only of the male (Murdo), none of this implies "that his actions and choices were uncaused or in principle unpredictable."[7] He further insists that, even if in the future psychologists and physiologists are able to predict such choices with perfect accuracy, still this would not show that he (Murdo) does not act freely.[8] For the case we have described is a perfect model (paradigm) of what the words acting freely actually mean. Therefore, "there is no contradiction involved in saying that a particular action or choice was: both free, and could have been helped and so on, *and* predictable, or even foreknown, and explicable in terms of caused causes."[9]

All that is necessary is that the chain of caused causes lead to a volition that is caused by some impulse or inclination which is grounded in the character of the agent, that character itself having been shaped by the sorts of causes we have in mind when we speak of training or education. For example, B.F. Skinner's model of shaping through conditioning might exemplify the sort of chain of causes Flew has in mind.[10]

We might note in passing that the traditional Christian apologist cannot look for comfort in the perhaps intuitively appealing notion that those human choices which exhibit free will are in principle unpredictable. For the main line of Christian orthodoxy has maintained that God can not only predict but foreknows everything that will happen in the world.

The Mackie and Flew challenge, if valid, shows that God could have attained his great goal in a world in which he would cause humans always to choose the good and to do so with free will. The validity of the Mackie and Flew argument, however, depends upon the validity of the determinist doctrine, and there is no way to decide if that doctrine is valid or not. Unfortunately, the attempts to refute Mackie and Flew by theologians have been formulated in such a way as to depend upon the refutation of the doctrine of determinism (and there is no way to do that either). That debate is undecidable.

Attempts to refute Mackie and Flew have relied primarily upon the contention that there is a logical contradiction in saying that an act is an act of free will and that it is fully determined by causes antecedent to the act of willing itself. Consider the refutation offered by Alvin Plantinga: "Now God can create free creatures, but He can't *cause* or *determine* them to do only what is right. For if He does so, then they aren't significantly free after all; they do not do what is right *freely*."[11]

Mackie and Flew insist that an act of the will that is completely determined can also be an act of free will; Plantinga maintains that it cannot. We should suspect that two different concepts of free will are at work and this is indeed the case. We have already considered Flew's description of a paradigm act of free will. The definition of free will given by Plantinga is quite different:

> If a person is free with respect to a given action, then he is free to perform that action and free to refrain from performing it; *no antecedent conditions and/or causal laws determine that he will perform that action, or that he won't.*[12]

This disagreement between Plantinga, and Mackie and Flew is indicative of the futility of much of the discussion of the free will defense by philosophers and theologians. The debate is doomed from the outset because there is no agreement on the concept of free will. This should perhaps not be too surprising, for each camp has supposed that free will cannot be described or defined except in reference to the issue of determinism versus indeterminism; and since that is an undecidable issue, no sound conclusion emerges from either camp. But it is a mistake to tie the concept of free will to the issue of determinism versus indeterminism. Fortunately the concept of free will can be made quite clear in a way that is neutral with regard to the determinism issue, as we shall see in the chapter 6.

Moreover, the disagreement between these three philosophers illustrates the need to recognize the four levels of the complex of abilities which constitute free will: an act of free will must be uncoerced, intentional, voluntary and autonomous (see chapter 6). With particular reference to the disagreement now under discussion, it is clear that Mackie and Flew have in mind what I have called moral free will, whereas Plantinga clearly has in mind what I have called autonomy.

THE DEBATE OVER DETERMINISM IS UNDECIDABLE

I have said that the debate over determinism versus indeterminism is undecidable. I want to say just a bit about this only because much effort has traditionally been given over to trying to settle the matter, in the conviction that it had to be decided in order to make clear what is implied by the concept of free will. Moreover, those theologians who have sought to refute Mackie and Flew have obviously thought that they could do so only if they could also refute the determinist position. For they insist that free will is not compatible with determinism, and they need to affirm that humans have or, in the case of the calvinist tradition, had free will so that they can argue that the free will defense, is sound.

I want very briefly to make three points on this topic. (1) As I show in chapter 6, it is quite possible to make clear the concept of free will, and to ascribe free will to humans, insofar as we are concerned with free will as a necessary condition for moral responsibility, without making any reference to either determinism or indeterminsim. (2) If this is correct, then there is no way to refute Mackie's and Flew's challenge to the free will defense, unless we can justify the claim that the sort of free will requisite for citizenship in the Kingdom of God involves not only moral responsibility for one's freely chosen actions but also involves autonomy. (3) We cannot settle the issue of determinism versus indeterminism, because in order to do so we would have to able to show that we have taken into consideration all of the factors which might legitimately count as having a causal influence upon any particular event, and this we cannot do. The sensible determinist does not claim that he or she can in fact demonstrate that event X was caused by such and such a complex and virtually infinite chain of prior events in such a way as to be predictable in advance, but only that in principle, if we knew all of the events in that chain, then we could have predicted X. And, of course, there is no way of disproving a counterfactual claim. Before leaving this point, however, I ought in fairness to the determinist position mention an argument commonly used to bolster their claims: namely, that even though we cannot account for all the causal factors that presumably determine an event, we can show that as we learn more about these factors, we increase the accuracy of our predictions. The suggestion is that, extrapolating from this, we could make completely accurate predictions, if we knew all of the causal factors. In any case, Mackie and Flew do not need, in order to bolster their attack upon the free will defense, to prove that determinism is the correct doctrine. They need only to show that there is no logical impossibility involved in the claims of determinism. For, if something is logically possible, the omnipotent God could, or could have, brought it about. Even if our actual world is not deterministic, God could have made it so, if no logical impossibility is involved. Mackie and Flew need also to show that there is no logical contradiction in affirming both determinism and free will (in the sense required in order to impute moral responsibility to agents). In this they seem to have allies within the theological camp of calvinism, and they seem as well to have produced some cogent arguments for their view.

CALVIN'S DIVINE DETERMINISM

There is one important type of Christian theology which has a number of affinities with the position we have called compatibilism, even though it is not identical with it. I refer to the theology of John Calvin. He had important predecessors; he seems, for example, to be a faithful follower of the later Augustine, especially in Augustine's anti-Pelagian writings. But my interest in discussing Calvin is not primarily historical. Even if compatibilism is an acceptable, or at least a nonrefutable, doctrine on philosophical grounds, and even if it can be reconciled with some traditional type of Christian theology (e.g. calvinism), it has implications for the concept of God, and of God's relation to the world, that are unacceptable on other grounds. That is, it must be rejected, if one is to be able to develop an adequate theodicy and also maintain an acceptable concept of God. This, of course, is simply another way of demonstrating that the challenge of Mackie and Flew is a very serious one indeed.

Calvinism shows that something very like compatibilism was developed within Christian theology long before our time. Calvinism also shows why and where compatibilism cannot be accommodated within any viable theodicy. In discussing calvinism, I want to set the issues of free will and determinism in the context of a somewhat broader understanding of Calvin's system, for there are other aspects of his theology which also pose very serious problems for theodicy. In other words, the very negative implications of compatibilism are not the only reason for rejecting calvinism.

Calvin's views differ from the compatibilism of Mackie and Flew in several respects. When Flew, for example, speaks of caused causes he has in mind natural causes, the sort, the might one day be embraced in laws discovered by physiologists and psychologists. Calvin holds that all events are determined by the will of God.[13] For this reason I call his system a divine determinism. Second, Mackie and Flew maintain that ordinary human beings exhibit free will in certain kinds of actions (e.g. in the paradigm case described by Flew). On the other hand, Calvin says that humans, after the Fall, unless they have been specially redeemed by the grace of God, utterly lost the capacity of free will. Nevertheless, Calvin agrees with Mackie and Flew on the point that is of crucial importance for the free will defense: namely, ordinary human beings, even those who are not redeemed, are morally responsible for those of their actions that are morally significant. For Calvin holds that humans are responsible for their sins, and justly punished for them, even though they do not possess free will, because they sin *voluntarily*.[14]

According to Calvin, all events whatsoever are not only foreseen but determined by the explicit will of God.[15] Even "the deliberations and volitions of men are so governed by his providence as to be directed to the end appointed by it."[16] Why then, we must ask, is not God responsible for the evil acts that men do? Is not God responsible for sin? The logic of divine determinsm seems to require an affirmative answer and Calvin, in one place, seems to agree God is the Author of evil.[17] But, of course, Calvin soon wants to take this back, and does so just a few pages later. Men do what is evil out of an evil motivation and for an evil end; God makes use of the instrumentality of evil men to do what is evil, but he does so out of a good and pure motivation and for a good end. "Hence, since the criminal misdeeds perpetrated by men proceed from God with a cause that is just, though perhaps unknown to us, though the first cause of all things is his will, I nevertheless deny that he is the Author of sin."[18]

It would seem, then, that a calvinist could well support the argument of Mackie and Flew, insofar as we consider only the logic of the argument. According to Calvin, God does in fact determine all events, including those that shape human character and the actions an agent performs. Those agents are nevertheless morally responsible for their actions. God could have brought it about that all human beings are wholly virtuous in such a way that it would be proper to praise them for their virtue.[19]

If one feels uncomfortable about identifying Calvin with the views of Mackie and Flew, as I do, it is because there remains a troubling ambiguity concerning the relationship between moral responsibility and free will. This ambiguity is evident in several things Calvin has to say about free will and moral responsibility. For one thing, there is an apparent inconsistency in Calvin's thought, and, second, his notion of a voluntary action needs to be specified more precisely. Moreover, Calvin requires (if he is to survive the Mackie and Flew attack) a notion that such actions are not only voluntary but autonomous. But the notion of autonomous actions in the sense required by the free will defense is incompatible with Calvin's divine determinism. Let us turn directly to his writings to illustrate and assess these problems.

As to the apparent inconsistency, Calvin asserts not only that Adam was created with a will that was sound and free[20] but that it is necessary to attribute free will to Adam and Eve, as originally created by God, for two reasons: (1) "lest in precisely pointing out the natural evils of men, we seem to refer them to the Author of nature," and (2) to deprive humans of all excuse for their sins.[21] Both these points imply that we may properly blame Adam rather than God for Adam's sin only if his sinful action was done with a free will. Yet, Calvin insists subsequent humans do not have free will, it having been utterly lost in the Fall, and yet he argues they are responsible and damnable for their sins. Calvin goes so far as to say that "the will, bereft of freedom, is of necessity either drawn or led into evil."[22] As noted earlier, he tries to resolve this apparent contradiction by saying that, though we sin necessarily, we sin *voluntarily*.

> Man, as he was corrupted by the Fall, sinned willingly, not unwillingly or by compulsion; by the most eager prompting of his own lust, not by compulsion from without. Yet so depraved is his nature that he can be moved or impelled only to evil.[23]

But if there is indeed a distinction between free and voluntary, as Calvin's explicit text indicates, then his earlier effort to excuse God and blame Adam for sin, on the grounds that Adam had free will, does not pass muster. Perhaps it is the case, if we wish to put the best face upon it, that Calvin's thought is uncharacteristically muddled.

I want to make another point the full force of which cannot be understood until we have completed the analysis of the concept of free will in chapter 6. Christian theologians, and most philosophers, for some reason, perhaps because of the prestige of Aristotle, argue that there are only two components, or conditions, of free will (i.e. to be an act of free will an act must be intentional and it must be uncoerced by any external force). They do not consider another essential condition: namely, that an act of free will must also be voluntary. When in chapter 6 we see what is meant by voluntary as a necessary condition for freedom of the will, we will also see that it cannot be reconciled with Calvin's description of a will that is, as he says, following St. Paul, in "bondage to sin,"[24] or a will that is, as he says, necessarily drawn or led into evil.

Our discussion of the difficulties in the calvinist view is still not finished. There are two other crucial points to be made. First, in seeking to extricate himself from the apparent contradiction noted above, Calvin falls back upon the doctrine of the solidarity of the human race in Adam, the notion that in Adam and his actions all humankind is implicated. I have already shown that this concept is unacceptable (see p. 17 above). Among other things, there are two moral objections to it: (1) that humans are blamed and horribly punished for sins not within their power to avoid, and (2) that humans are punished for the sin of someone other than themselves. I would like also to suggest what seems to me the only plausible motive behind such a ploy on Calvin's part. It is, of course, to exonerate God from all responsibility for evil. Later I want to suggest that an even adequate free will defense does not do this.

The other objection that should be mentioned is that the whole scheme, of which this damnation for total depravity stemming from original sin is part, seems to imply a concept of God which is morally abhorrent. Let us grant, for the sake of argument, but contrary to the objection made above, that all humans subsequent to Adam are in bondage to sin, that they sin necessarily, and that they are therefore justly damnable. According to Calvin, God out of his mere mercy and grace rescues some from this depravity and damnation. Those elected to salvation are chosen by the secret counsel of God and, so far as we can know, wholly arbitrarily. They are no more worthy of redemption than any others. The question then arises with urgency: why does not God extend his mercy and grace to all humans? Calvin has two answers to this question: it is presumptuous and blasphemous to ask it[25] and it is necessary that there be some who suffer just condemnation and eternal punishment in order that God may "show ... what the verdict of his justice could do".[26]

While it may be just to punish those whose acts of free will are evil, it is perverse and reprehensible that God should punish (and with such ferocity) those who have no free will and who cannot not sin.

Given calvinism, then, there is no way to refute the attacks of Mackie and Flew. To do so we need to insist that the sort of free will, which is requisite to citizenship in the Kingdom of God, includes an autonomy that is incompatible with the views of Mackie and Flew or Calvin. In Calvin's system, human actions are caused by God and therefore are not autonomous. Autonomy also implies human intellectual freedom, and Calvin also denies the right of humans to question the ways of God.

ALTERNATIVES WITHIN CHRISTIAN THEOLOGY

I wanted to say a good deal about the theology of John Calvin because his system illustrates the fact that something very like the compatibilism which is the foundation of Mackie's and Flew's attack on the free will defense has been defended by influential thinkers within the Christian tradition. It is worth noting (even if it is so well known as to be scarcely necessary) that on the points we have discussed above, Calvin's view is by no means representative of the whole Christian tradition. In fact, it represents a minority point of view. The development and defense of my own version of the free will defense requires a noncalvinist view: namely, that free will in the full sense requisite for citizenship in the Kingdom of God includes autonomy of the will, and it is logically impossible that our wills should be autonomous and yet be caused to function in this way or that by God or by any external force. In those choices of the autonomous will, its volitions are independent of the will of God. Since this is not a treatise in historical theology, it is not necessary for me to cite the many supports for my point of view in the tradition. I will say a word about three theologians, whose ideas suggest the direction I think we should move in.

Thomas Aquinas (d.1274 A.D.), whose views on these matters are closer to the mainline tradition than are those of Calvin, could be cited at length but I content myself with a few references. Aquinas' notion of divine providence seems at first little if at all different from that of Calvin.

God's will, he says, "is the universal cause of all things and cannot but achieve its effect."[27] He insists, however, that neither God's providence nor his predestining activity imposes necessity upon all things. For God has explicitly willed that some things should come about by necessity and other things through the free choice of rational agents. If God wills a thing, it is bound to be. But it does not follow from this that those things chosen by free will are chosen by necessity, for God wills that these things come about contingently. Aquinas also states quite clearly that rational agents must possess free will if they are to be held morally responsible for their actions.[28] And Aquinas is more consistent in applying this requirement than is Calvin, since he says that, if humans subsequent to Adam are to be held responsible for their actions, they, too, must possess free will; therefore, the Fall did not result in the utter loss of free will but only in its weakening.[29]

Support for the notion that the human will is free in the sense of being autonomous is not confined to the Roman Catholic tradition. To cite only one influential Protestant thinker, I mention briefly the relevant views of Kierkegaard (d. 1855 A.D.). In Kierkegaard, I find someone even closer to the views I wish to put forward, since, as I note, he associates this freedom of the will with a process of self-development.

According to Kierkegaard, one must become a self before one can become a Christian (i.e., can choose faith in God). The entire text of his Sickness Unto Death is a complex description of the task of becoming a self, which is a task for the whole of one's life.[30] Prior to the leap of faith by which one chooses God, it is necessary one choose to exist as an ethical individual, which Kierkegaard describes as becoming subjective.[31] Just as the ethical mode of life requires freely choosing to obey the ethical imperative, so our choice of God must be made in autonomy; indeed, in order that we may have that autonomy, our relation to God must be subjective. This means his communication with us will be indirect—inviting, not compelling.

> To communicate in this manner constitutes the most beautiful triumph
> of the resigned inwardness. And therefore no one is so resigned as God;
> for he communicates in creating, so as by creating to give independence
> over against himself.[32]

This self-limitation on the part of God, so that we may choose God freely, is precisely the point of the lengthy parable of the King, who loves a humble maiden, which we find in another work.[33] One final passage from Kierkegaard speaks so directly to these matters that it deserves quotation at some length. In *Training in Christianity* he is at one point commenting on *John* 12:32, "And I, if I be lifted up from the earth, will draw all unto myself." Kierkegaard continues:

> What is meant by drawing unto itself depends upon the nature of what is drawn. If it is in itself a self, then the phrase "to draw truly to oneself" cannot mean merely to draw it away from being its own self, to draw it in such a way that it loses its own existence. ... No, when that which is to be drawn is itself a self, the real meaning of truly drawing to itself is, first to help it become truly its own self, so as then to draw in to oneself, or it means to help it become its own self with and by the drawing it to oneself. What is it then to be a self? ... But a self is a duplication; it is freedom: hence in this case "drawing truly to oneself" means to present a choice.[34]

Mention must also be made of Irenaeus (d. 202 A.D.). Though he became Bishop of Lyons, France, he came from Smyrna, and it is chiefly in the Eastern Orthodox tradition where his thought has its greatest influence. Indeed, he is to this day regarded as one of the chief fountainheads of Orthodoxy. Many of his ideas are suggestive of the approach to the free will defense I find most persuasive. Irenaeus holds humans learn gradually through their own experience of good and evil how to distinguish between good and evil and freely choose good. Though Irenaeus agrees with virtually all of the theologians who espouse the tradition that God created Adam and Eve with free will, it is clear that this is thought of as a potentiality that must be developed. "God made man a free agent from the beginning, possessing his own power, even as he does his own soul, to obey the behest of God voluntarily and not by compulsion of God."[35]

Of great importance is Irenaeus' distinction between the image and the likeness of God. *Gen.* 1:26 reads, "Then God said, 'Let us make man in our image, after our likeness. ...'" According to Irenaeus, the image refers to the fact that we have rational and moral capacities to become like God, but these are potentialities, which must be developed into the actual likeness to God's rationality and righteousness. Man is born immature and imperfect, and only through this spiritual development can he attain the perfection of God.[36]

In a passage that clearly refers not just to Adam and Eve but to humankind generally this theme of development through learning is specified. Humans, Irenaeus says, must:

> come to know both the good of obedience and the evil of disobedience, that the eye of the mind, receiving experience of both, may with

judgment make choice of the better things. ... How, if he had no knowledge of the contrary, could he have had instruction in that which is good? ... If anyone do shun the knowledge of both these kinds of things, and the twofold perception of knowledge, he unawares divests himself of the character of a human being. How then shall he be a God, who has not yet been made a man? Or how can he be perfect who was but lately created? ... For it must be that thou, at the outset, shouldest hold the rank of a man, and then afterwards partake of the glory of God. ... If, then, thou art God's workmanship, await the hand of thy Maker, which creates everything in due time; in due time as far thou art concerned, whose creation is being carried out.[37]

SUMMARY

The upshot is that the attack by Professors Mackie and Flew on Christian theodicy and Christian theology generally, and the attempts of theologians to refute it, illustrate the need for a more adequate concept of free will than has traditionally been employed. Also, the efforts to refute Mackie and Flew cannot succeed if one continues to uphold the sort of traditional notions of divine omnipotence and providence, which imply that God does, or could determine by his own power and will all events that occur.

Chapter 4

Should the Traditional Free Will Defense Be Revised?

It seems that the traditional free will defense is in need of revision, but there are many who resist such a notion, and many more yet who will object to the revisions I will eventually suggest—revisions which will seem to many traditionalists extreme and as an abandonment of the Christian faith altogether.

In this brief chapter I want, first, to list in summary form, the problems with the traditional free will defense that seem to require revisions. (These problems have already been raised in previous chapters.) Second, I want to present my own reasons for regarding such revisionism as warranted, even for one who wishes to remain within the bounds of the Christian faith.

Summary of Problems with the Traditional Free Will Defense

1. The attack mounted by Professors Mackie and Flew cannot be positively refuted unless one can refute their doctrine of compatibilism and the causal determinism upon which it is based. And there is no way of disproving determinism (see pp. 23–24). There *is* an alternative to determinism, which is more plausible though not itself provable, but this alternative has not been articulated clearly in most traditional theodicies. This shortcoming is due, in part, to the fact that an adequate concept of free will has not developed within the tradition; I shall try to remedy that shortcoming. In my last chapter, I present what I consider a plausible nondeterministic view of acts that are done with free will.

2. That part of the tradition which is illustrated by the theologies of Luther and Calvin exhibits the sort of divine determinism that fits well with Mackie's and Flew's compatibilism and, therefore, cannot refute the attack of the latter upon traditional theodicy. Moreover, this line of the tradition is, as we have seen, open to other serious objections.

3. The so-called contrast theory that which is prominent in traditional forms of theodicy, is unconvincing unless it is an integral part of an adequate free will defense. And such a free will defense cannot be adequate if it includes the traditional notion of divine omnipotence. For, even given the necessity of granting free will to humans, and granting that, having done so, God cannot prevent humans from misusing their free will; nevertheless, a God who is omnipotent, as conceived in traditional terms, could have arranged things so that the world contained fewer and less grievous evils.

4. The fact that the tradition does not make use of an adequate concept of free will has given rise to a number of problems, most often characterized by lack of clarity or just plain confusion.

5. Theologians in the western traditions of the church found it necessary to invoke doctrines concerning the sin and the fall of Adam and Eve, and the doctrine of the transmission of sinfulness to all subsequent humans. This seemed necessary in order to account for the wretched and universal sinfulness of humanity, and for the fact that it could be reconciled to God in no other way than through the atoning death of Jesus Christ. Though motivated out of this christological and soteriological concern, this set of ideas is unwarranted and in at least one regard self-contradictory. (a) It is said that Adam and Eve must have possessed free will in choosing to disobey God, otherwise the blame would fall not upon them but upon God (see p. 26). Yet subsequent humans, who have either utterly lost their free will (as in Luther and Calvin), or have had it so weakened as to be ineffectual without God's special grace (as in Thomas Aquinas), are nevertheless held responsible and damnable for their condition of sinfulness. (b) Adam and Eve, as depicted in the Bible, lacked the conditions which are necessary for the development of free will (see p. 17). Therefore, they could not be morally responsible for their act, and certainly not for an act depicted as being so heinously wicked as is required by the traditional doctrines of original and originating sin. They were in a condition more like that of innocent children (as the eastern tradition maintains), still needing to learn through experience those things necessary before one can possess free will and be fully responsible in morally significant actions. (c) If it were the case that *all* subsequent humans are sinful in such a way as to merit damnation, and if it is only through an arbitrary gift of grace that some are redeemed, then why does God not extend that grace to all? There is no

good answer to that question in the traditional theodicies. The answer given by Calvin (see p. 28) implies that God has a character which is morally repugnant!

It will be possible to give further support to the criticisms of the traditional accounts of the Adam and Eve defection after a more adequate concept of free will has been developed in chapter 6. Though these criticisms imply a need for revisions of the traditional free will defense, there is a further question of whether revisions can be made while still remaining within the parameters of the Christian faith.

REVISIONISM AND THE CHRISTIAN FAITH

When I discuss the revisions that I believe are needed, with friends who consider themselves to be staunch and true Christians, I very often get decidedly negative reactions ranging from raised eyebrows and wrinkled brows to stern admonitions that I am in grave danger of heresy. I am told that what I propose is many ways contrary to Christian faith. Perhaps so. Certainly it runs counter to a number of doctrines that have characterized mainline Christian tradition during much of its history.

But I maintain not only that the revisions I propose are necessary if the free will defense is to be strengthened but that it can be demonstrated that the Christian faith has always been in process of revision. That claim, about constant revisionism, may be challenged by some, but the challenge depends upon a certain sort of exclusive dogmatism. My claim regarding revisionism will no doubt be rejected by those who maintain that they alone possess the authentic version of the Christian faith as it was formulated in Apostolic times, as it has been preserved without change, and as guaranteed by the text of a Bible that is absolutely without error.

But if one looks at the major mainline Christian strands, and studies the theologies they have produced, one sees a considerable variety of views on many central doctrines, and finds it difficult, if not impossible, to draw tight and distinct bounds around the Christian faith. Moreover, even within a single strand, which exhibits historical continuity, one can discern changes in important ways of understanding elements of the Christian faith.

I would be willing to settle for the notion that in order to consider oneself within the parameters of the Christian faith one must believe that "God was in Christ reconciling the world to himself."[1] But how was God in Christ? It took the church fathers five centuries to come to agreement on that, and soon after the end of the Council of Chalcedon, in which the final component of that agreement was reached, a wide variety of opinions arose as to how the words of the Creed were to be interpreted. How was that reconciliation effected? Eventually, after much quarreling over this issue, an orthodox line established the notion of Christ's substitutionary atonement as the chief explanation; but there continued to be a group, who certainly regarded themselves as Christians, who preferred the notion of atonement through moral suasion, and whose line of thought has remained vital to the present day. Was the whole world reconciled, or only a select few? Those who opted for the notion of a universal salvation, and there were many, were eventually branded as heretics, but that line of thought has continued.[2]

Think of the great changes in the concept of God that arose from the assimilation of Greek (especially Platonic) ideas into the thinking of the church fathers. I have in mind especially the notion that God is completely unchanging in every respect, a notion, which dominated all Christian thought from the second century onward, and still is, unfortunately, the majority view. This led to some ideas that seem radically different from the ideas about God which prevail in the Bible. For example, many theologians denied that God in reality ever feels compassion, for to feel compassion implies a change in the one who is compassionate.[3] One who is compassionate is changed by the suffering of one for whom he or she cares. One could quote innumerable passages of Scripture which clearly indicate the compassion of God, none more eloquently than chapter 11 of Hosea.[4]

Think of the shock and dismay among the Roman Catholics of the medieval period when Albertus Magnus and Thomas Aquinas began to use Aristotelian concepts to interpret many central Christian doctrines. They even explicated their views regarding the existence and the nature of God with the aid of Aristotelian concepts. At the University of Paris, the writings of Aristotle were condemned and burned. Yet it did not take long before the writings of Thomas Aquinas were generally regarded as the most definitive exposition of Christian theology![5]

The antirevisionists are also on shaky ground if they appeal to the Bible. Fundamentalist christians maintain that the Bible, being the veritable Word of God, contains *clearly* and authoritatively the definitive truth on all essential matters of the Christian faith. Yet, if biblical texts are read with an undogmatic mind, so far as possible, it is clear one finds a variety of views regarding many central religious ideas, including conflicting ideas. In the heyday of liberalism it was thought that one could discern an evolution of ideas within the texts, an evolution from the more primitive to the more enlightened, or from the religion of the Old Testament to the religion of Jesus.[6] In chapter 5 I shall have something to say about variations, and apparent discrepancies, in texts dealing with the concept of the power of God. The point I make here may perhaps be most appropriately illustrated by looking at some of the variations in the biblical texts concerning the understanding of the nature of God. And it will suffice to mention a variation that is quite radical, suggesting as it does an outright contradiction.

A number of biblical texts which undoubtedly date from an early period characterize God as a God of war. In the so-called "Song of Moses," we are told "Yahweh is a man of war; Yahweh is his name."[7] On the day God caused the sun to stand still so as to give complete victory to Joshua and his troops, Joshua had no doubt that "Yahweh fought for Israel."[8]

Not only is Yahweh a God of war, but a ruthless one. In the war against the Amalekites, the prophet Samuel delivers to Saul the words of the Lord, and Saul is instructed that God will punish Amalek through Saul and his troops which are to "go and smite Amalek, and utterly destroy all that they have; do not spare them, but kill both man and woman, infant and suckling, ox and sheep, camel and ass."[9] But, alas, Saul spared Agag and the best of the cattle.[10] For such disobedience Saul is fiercely denounced and informed that his rule as king will be ended.[11]

This view of God as a God of war is accompanied by an extremely tribalistic view of the covenant. Yahweh says, "I will be an enemy to your enemies, and an adversary to your adversaries."[12] This view is completely changed in the understanding of the great prophets. According to Isaiah, Yahweh will use Assyria as the rod of his anger to punish Israel for her sins.[13] Perhaps the clearest change is evident in the prophecy of Amos, who proclaimed a universal standard of justice, based on the will of Yahweh, for all nations, and who announces that Israel will be punished double for her sins, precisely because Israel has had the privilege of receiving the ethical covenant. The entire book of Amos should be consulted, for it all supports the conclusion he reaches and announces in the name of the Lord: "Are you not like the Ethiopians to me, O people of Israel?"[14]

In the very earliest period in the development of Christianity this prophetic insight and universalism was adopted. The disciples are to go to all nations to preach and to baptize. And it seems to me that in our own day there is a strong trend towards a universalism with regard to God's saving grace. One can find this, not only amongst the Universalists, whose hallmark this notion was from the beginning of their movement, but even amongst Roman Catholics, though not quite so boldly and clearly. One finds this trend reflected in the Documents of Vatican II, in the notion of baptism by desire. Even those who know nothing of Jesus Christ may receive the saving grace of God if they honor God according to their own best understanding and strive to live a righteous life![15]

With all of this in mind can we, then, rule out as heretical the sorts of modifications that I find to be necessary? They are less radical than some of those I have mentioned above.

Chapter 5

The Concept of a Limited God

In the mainline tradition of Christian thought the free will defense is set in the context of a theology which conceives of God as omnipotent. In most of the attacks upon the free will defense this doctrine of omnipotence has played a prominent role. The line of attack usually takes something like the following form: if God is truly omnipotent (or, indeed, if there be such a reality as an omnipotent God) then he could have arranged it so that there would be no evils; or, an omnipotent God could have arranged it so that humans would have free will and yet be so constituted in a world so constituted that there would be no evils, or at least fewer and less grievous evils.

The connections between the doctrine of omnipotence and the problems it raises for the free will defense have been evident in our earlier chapters, perhaps in greatest detail in chapter 3 in which the challenge of Mackie and Flew is considered. *It is my view that the traditional notion of God's omnipotence, in spite of all of the ingenious efforts to reconcile it with the sort of human free will required by the free will defense, makes it impossible to rebut the attacks of Professors Flew and Mackie, and, moreover, makes it clear that God is ultimately responsible for the evils of the world.*

In this chapter I examine the traditional doctrine insofar as it is relevant for our discussion of the free will defense and to show why I have come to this conclusion. This will also require a look at traditional (and in my view futile) efforts to maintain the doctrine of omnipotence, while at the same time striving to couple it with some sort of notion of the limitation of God's power. The very fact that traditional theologians have felt compelled to add something about the limitations of God's power should, I think, be taken as an indication of their own recognition of the cogency of the conclusion stated above.

It is not surprising that these problems, which attend the doctrine of omnipotence, have led a number of thinkers to develop the notion of a limited God. There is, as we shall see, one view regarding such a limitation that has been incorporated into the orthodox tradition, namely, the notion that God has freely limited his own power in relation to morally significant human decisions. In general and apart from this tamed version, these efforts have been treated with scorn by more orthodox theologians. They have been regarded as totally unacceptable deviations from the Christian faith.

In this present chapter I want to argue that, so far as the free will defense is concerned, there is already in the tradition, though not quite as explicitly and clearly as I should like, a notion of the limitation upon God's power which has seemed adequate and necessary to the vast majority of free will defenders. This notion is not accepted by all branches of Christian theology; those who disagree are clearly in the minority and clearly find even greater difficulties in dealing with the problems mentioned above. The minority view I refer to is that held, for example, by Calvin (see pp. 24–28). Even within the Lutheran tradition, however, things had shifted considerably, as early as the influential work of Melanchthon,[1] in the direction of the majority view. And today it is increasingly difficult to find, even in the tradition founded by Calvin, a defender of his divine determinism.

I say that the view which has been accepted in the mainline of the tradition has seemed adequate to its supporters. However, we shall see that this view is far from clear and it is very doubtful that it serves the purpose of reconciling the notion of divine omnipotence with the sort of free will necessary to the free will defense.

Nor will this majority of free will defenders be pleased with another point I want to make: namely, that even with this commonly accepted notion of the limitation on God's power, the free will defender is still left with serious residual problems. In my final, and rather speculative chapter (chapter 8), I suggest the desirability and feasibility of a more radical notion of a limitation upon God's power.

A Traditional Notion of the Limitation of God's Power

The traditional notion that I have in mind goes like this: though God's power is essentially unlimited, nevertheless God has freely limited his own power in order to make possible human free will and moral responsibility. In human actions that are morally significant, God does not intervene to determine what is done but leaves it to the free and autonomous decision of the human moral agent. This view is seldom stated as baldly as I have just done. Moreover, it is usually accompanied by qualifications that quite frankly to amount to double-talk. The sort of qualifications I have in mind make it quite unclear whether in the final analysis this free and autonomous decision of the human moral agent is not over-ridden by the will of God in such a way as to deprive it of autonomy. Nevertheless, the development of the concept of the self-limitation of God's power testifies to the fact that Christian theodicy, with regard to the problem of moral evil, requires some sort of limitation.

I want first to articulate the well-established view of the self-limitation of God's power and then briefly cite passages that muddy and confuse this view. I do this by citing passages of Thomas Aquinas, who in his day summarized the traditional wisdom on these matters and whose views have dominated since. And then I summarize views on this topic from a recent edition of *The Catholic Encyclopedia*, which at least to my mind, show that the effort to reconcile the doctrines of divine omnipotence and divine providence with the attribution of moral free will to humans has not led to a clear or cogent result.

THOMAS AQUINAS ON PROVIDENCE, OMNIPOTENCE AND FREE WILL

The will of God must needs always be fulfilled.[2]
God's will is unchangeable.[3]

As to things willed by God, we must observe that He wills some things of absolute necessity; but this is not true of all that He wills. ... But God wills things apart from Himself in so far as they are ordered to His own goodness as their end. Now in willing the end we do not necessarily will things that conduce to it, unless they are such that the end cannot be attained without them. ... Yet it (God's will) can be necessary by supposition, for supposing that He wills a thing, then He is unable not to will it, as His will cannot change.[4]

Rational creatures are masters of their own acts, and for this reason certain expressions of the divine will are assigned to their acts, inasmuch as God ordains rational creatures to act voluntarily and of themselves. Other creatures act only as moved by the divine operation.[5]

Since a rational creature has, through its free will, control over its actions ... it is subject to divine providence in an especial manner, so that something is imputed to it as a fault, or as a merit, and there is given it according something by way of punishment or reward.[6]

Man has free will: otherwise counsels, exhortations, commands, prohibitions, rewards, punishments would be in vain.[7]

And by a special favor, it was granted him [Adam] that no creature outside himself could harm him against his own will, whereby he was able even to resist the temptation of the demon.[8]

It is all of this I have in mind when I say that there has long been in the tradition a concept of the self-limitation of God's omnipotence, of God's freely limiting his own power in order to make room for human free will and moral responsibility. I am justified in inferring a very probable motive for this line of thought; namely, only if something like this view is correct can it seem that God is blameless for the evils in the world and the blame be placed upon humans.

This notion of a self-limitation of God's power strengthens the free will defense. We also see it still leaves some serious problems and that a more radical notion of the limitation upon God's power is ultimately required.

Before leaving the topic of this long held traditional notion of the limitation on God's power, however, I want to point out that, though it seems useful to the free will defender, that usefulness is considerably diminished by the fact that it is finally rendered unclear by what these theologians had to say about God's providence and omnipotence. They felt the need to attribute free will to humans but they evidently feared that this would detract too much from God's providence and power. So they equivocate. Some of the relevant passages indicate that human free will is in fact overruled by the divine will (though I admit that this is not altogether clear). And the reason it is not clear is that the theologians indulge in such supersophisticated distinction-making and metaphysical jargon, that no clear message comes through. It is this sort of thing, and I cite but a few of the passages, again from Thomas Aquinas, which illustrate the equivocation and lack of clarity.

A distinction is made between the "antecedent will" of God and the "consequent" will of God. This distinction must not be taken as applying to the divine will itself, in which there is neither antecedent or consequent, but rather to things willed.... A thing taken in its primary sense may be good or evil, and yet when some additional circumstances are taken into account, by a consequent consideration, may be changed into the opposite. ... God antecedently wills all men to be saved, but consequently wills some to be damned, as His justice exacts.[9]

Since this distinction "must not be taken as applying to the divine will itself" and since the divine will cannot be changed, it certainly seems as if we can derive from this the following, namely, that God wills that some be damned and since God's will is always fulfilled and is unchangeable it would seem that some (including particular individuals) will necessarily be damned as God wills. Where in all of this is free will? "Since the very act of free will is traced to God as a cause, it necessarily follows that everything happening from the exercise of free will must be subject to the divine providence."[10]

> Wherefore, it (divine providence) moves all things in accordance with their conditions; so that from necessary causes through the divine motion, effects follow of necessity; but from contingent causes effects follow contingently. Since, therefore, the will is an active principle not determined to one thing, God so moves it that He does not determine it of necessity to one thing, but its movement remains contingent and not necessary, except in those things to which it is moved naturally.[11]
>
> God wills whatever is required for a thing that He wills. ... But it befits certain things, according to the mode of their nature, that they be contingent and not necessary. Therefore, God wills that some things be contingent. Now the efficacy of the divine will requires not only that something be that God wills to be, but also that it be as He wills it to be.[12]
>
> *If God wills something, it will be.* But the consequent does not have to be necessary.[13]

From the words "the efficacy of the divine will requires...that something be that God wills to be" we may infer that, if God wills that some particular thing, even though it be contingent, occur in the future, it will necessarily come to be. We no doubt consider it to be a matter of contingency as to whether Jones will mow his grass next Saturday. But God knows eternally and infallibly precisely what Jones will do. And surely God's knowledge is knowledge of things as they really are and really will be. How then can what Jones will do be in reality a matter of contingency? How can Jones not do whatever it is that God knows that he will do? How, then, can we attribute free will to Jones? Here, as in many places, the theological waters run deep indeed—and are quite murky.

In more than seven hundred years since the death of Thomas Aquinas, this issue, the relationship between divine providence and human free will, has been continuously discussed, disputed, and puzzled over. Much of this discussion, especially within Roman Catholic circles, has referred back to the writings of Thomas Aquinas. It is not surprising, I think, that several schools of interpretation have arisen, nor that with all of this erudite pondering the problem still remains vexed and unresolved. By way of illustrating this conclusion, I consider some passages from *The Catholic Encyclopedia.*

The conclusion that even in Thomas Aquinas and the Catholic tradition we find a sort of divine determinism is further suggested by both the thomistic and generally orthodox Christian view of the relationship between God's knowledge and temporal events. God does not exist in time. The future and the past are alike ever present to the eternal mind. And the intuitive vision of God apprehends simultaneously what is future to us with all it contains. Furthermore, God's omnipotent providence exercises complete and perfect control over all events that happen or will happen in the universe.

If God, whose knowledge is perfect and unchangeable, infallibly and truly knows eternally all future events including what we in the ignorance of our finite knowledge call contingent events how can those future events not be determined? What will happen with regard to any event whatever is already determined. It is already known in all its specificity by God.

Since the time of Thomas Aquinas there have been within the Catholic tradition two major interpretations of his thought on this topic.

The thomistic (Benedictine) solution explains that God premoves each person in all of his or her acts to the line of conduct that he or she subsequently adopts. This premotive decree inclines a person's will with absolute certainty to the side decreed. This premotion, however, does not impose necessity on the person for God moves a person who is by nature a free cause to choose what he or she chooses. Such is the explanation. What an explanation! A person's will acts as a free cause that is inclined with absolute certainty to the side which God has determined. With all due respect to the honest intentions of these theologians, I cannot refrain from calling this double-talk and sophistry.

The Molinists (Jesuits) fare no better. They say that God does not premove the will but acts upon the human will concurrently. God's knowledge of what a free being would choose, if the necessary conditions were supplied, must be deemed logically prior to any decree of concurrence with respect to that act of choice. But, of course, God knows eternally precisely which necessary conditions will or will not be supplied. Molinists say that God knows future contingent events in his middle knowledge. He knows what will happen if certain conditions are supplied. But it is God who will supply whatever conditions will impinge upon all future events. And unless we suppose, per impossible, that God is ignorant of his own intentions, then God already knows (eternally knows) precisely what events will occur in the future—which, of course, leads to the same problematical conclusion we observed in the case of the Thomists.[14]

In summary, with regard to this long established orthodox view regarding the limitations on God's power, we see:

1. That it was felt necessary to hold the view that God limits his own power so that humans may have free will with regard to moral matters and themselves be responsible for the evils of the world.
2. Even if this idea is weakened by certain equivocation, it still stands as evidence of the need for some such limitation in the interests of Christian theodicy.
3. This long held orthodox view helps strengthen the free will defense.
4. In spite of this orthodox view, we are left with a number of serious problems, because (a) the equivocations weaken this traditional view; (b) the lack of clarity in this traditional view is further evidence of the futility of trying to explicate and defend the concept of free will by settling the issue of determinism versus indeterminism; and (c) even if we grant that it bolsters the free will defense as strongly as has been traditionally thought, it still leaves the free will defense open to very serious objections.

How and to what Extent this Traditional Notion Helps

This traditional majority view, assuming its cogency, helps the free will defender insofar as it supports the view that humans are responsible for moral evils and that God is not responsible for them. In fact, it is pretty clear this view was developed precisely for that purpose. To many, it explains why God logically cannot limit the amount of evil that humans bring about because of their misuse of their free will. If God intervenes to prevent evils then the human wills that initiate those evils are not free. But the implications of the traditional notion of divine omnipotence are such that this additional benefit cannot in fact be justly claimed.

As to the cogency of this traditional view, there are four main difficulties in the way it has been articulated:

1. It has included the notion that, precisely in order that he might be responsible, Adam was created with free will. After I have developed the concept of free will in chapter 6, we will see free will is not the sort of thing that can just be given to anybody, certainly not to anybody whose situation in life is like that biblically and traditionally attributed to Adam.

2. This traditional view does nothing to alleviate the great problem of natural evils.

3. Not all evils can be traced to the misuse of free will by humans, unless one takes the extraordinarily dubious and ad hoc line suggested by Augustine: namely, that before the sin of Adam there were no natural evils, but these arose as punishments for human sin.

4. Among other things, in order to deny there were natural evils long before humans appeared on the scene, one would have to repudiate the work and findings of modern geology, archaeology, and biology.

There is another problem with this traditional notion regarding the limits of God's power. Even granting this traditional view, insofar as it posits the self-limitation of divine power in order to make room for human free will and posits the view that moral evils have arisen from the misuse of that free will, nevertheless, given the traditional view of divine omnipotence, God could have arranged everything so that there would be far fewer and less grievous evils (see pp. 69–71).

Finally, this majority view has been qualified and muddied by dubious sophistry, so as to be unclear. Moreover, it would seem that the qualifications introduced to protect the doctrines of divine omnipotence and divine providence lead to something very like, if not identical with, the notion of divine determinism, which I have criticized elsewhere.

Finally, all of this indicates that the doctrine of divine omnipotence must be qualified in a more radical way than is provided in the thomistic and molinist views. I shall provide such a revision in chapter 8.

Chapter 6

The Concept of Free Will

A PRELIMINARY SKETCH

Free will, in the sense that is relevant to our inquiry, is a complex and learned ability—the ability to exercise rational control over one's volitions. I shall draw upon and adapt the analysis of this ability as developed by Professors Timothy Duggan and Bermard Gert. According to Duggan and Gert, an act of free will must be uncoerced, intentional, and voluntary.[1] Since this ability is complex and, as we shall see, a matter of degree, it is not surprising that there are certain mental acts that have often been regarded as acts of free will but fail to fully exemplify the ability that exists and is essential to the free will defense. For example, the mental act of intentionally choosing X rather than Y, when there is no compelling reason, motive, or incentive to choose either and when the choice is uncoerced, has often been regarded as an act of free will. I have no objection to this. I choose brussels sprouts rather than cabbage to go along with my veal cutlet, or I choose my brown jacket rather than my blue to wear to the picnic.

But the sort of free will that is essential to the free will defense is, in addition, morally significant. It is the sort of action for which one may appropriately be praised or blamed. Essential to the traditional free will defense is the claim that evils came into the world, and continue to do so, because of the wrongful (sinful) choices of free rational agents (angels and humans). So, while I do not wish to exclude what might from a moral point of view be called insignificant acts of free will, my discussion focuses

47

on what might be called morally significant acts of free will, or more simply, the moral free will.

We must also take note of another aspect or level, if we are to characterize the concept of free will in the most developed sense requisite for citizenship in the Kingdom of God. In addition to the necessary conditions mentioned above, such a will must be autonomous. An act performed by an autonomous will is one in which the agent reacts to antecedent causes in a selective, novel, and unpredictable way, and the principle of selectivity is internal to the psyche of the agent in the very moment of choice and no antecedent cause or cases function as sufficient cause for the choice.[2] This addition is necessary because there is no way to cope with the attack upon the free will defense made by Mackie and Flew (as noted in chapter 3) if we accept their doctrine of compatibilism, and there is no good reason why compatibilists cannot accept the view that acts of free will must be intentional, uncoerced, and voluntary. The claim that persons exercising the fullest and highest form of free will act with autonomy is not strictly provable but it is necessary to the free will defense, and it is, when properly formulated, a reasonable claim (see chapter 8). The addition of this condition is not, however, simply an ad hoc maneuver to meet the challenge of Mackie and Flew.

A crucial point in the analysis of this chapter arises over the question of whether intentionality, which is a necessary condition for free will, must rise to the level of deliberation between alternatives. I maintain such deliberation is crucial to free will in the fullest sense of the term, in the sense which is required, and for people who are fit to become citizens of the Kingdom of God. But many philosophers have maintained that deliberation is not essential that acts of genuine free will may be spontaneous. Here I rely on the contention that free will is a matter of degree, and my analysis will bear this out. Again, I have no objection to labeling spontaneous acts (so long as they are also uncoerced, intentional, and voluntary) as acts of free will, but I maintain they do not exemplify the highest or fullest type of free will. They do not rise to the level of that sort of rational control that enables a person to alter habitual or spontaneous actions in the light of new circumstances or new evidence.

Rational control implies the ability to remain flexible in one's actions and to choose what one really wants to choose in the light of an up-to-the-minute awareness of conditions and likely consequences. Thus, the reflection that is involved in the intentionality of free will is in principle without a limit—though existential considerations constrain every rational agent ultimately to set a limit and to act in a timely fashion.

The ability that is free will is complex because it is dependent upon and proportional to several other abilities:

1. The ability to control one's desires, so that one has the desires one wants to have upon reflection.
2. The ability to recognize and properly assess incentives both for doing and for not doing actions of various kinds.
3. The ability to both adjust one's beliefs to evidence and change one's beliefs when required by new evidence of sufficient weight. I want to approach a description of these abilities through discussion of the conditions that must obtain before properly judging an act to be an act of free will. It is important for us to know what these conditions are, since the absence of any one of them means that an action is not an act of free will, and such an absence may also provide an excuse, absolving one of moral responsibility for the act.

Careful consideration of these conditions will provide adequate understanding of the concept of free will as the ability to exercise rational control over one's volitions.

From this brief characterization, it is clear the ability of free will can develop only in the context of rational capabilities (presumably innate) and a considerable body of well-founded beliefs. The capacity or potentiality is present at birth, but the ability is not. It requires a long and complex learning process. That this is the case becomes more apparent as we discuss in more detail the conditions that are necessary for the development of this set of abilities.

FREE WILL IS A MENTAL ACT

"Willing," says Augustine, "is a movement of the mind, no one compelling either for not losing or for obtaining something."[3] He might well have added "or for avoiding something."

It seems that this movement of the mind is not absolutely unique to human minds and that among the movements of human minds are various sorts to be considered. The lion smells the gazelle and begins to stalk with a definite goal in mind. The human infant is aware of a patch of bright color and moves his hand to grasp it. John reaches his right hand up to scratch an itchy place behind his ear. Mary puts the cat out the back door before going to the office. Arthur very carefully places on the table all of the paraphernalia he will need for his injection of heroin. Susan writes out the invitations to a cocktail party to be given to introduce to friends her favorite candidate for mayor. All of these seem to be movements of the mind and instances of willing. But which of them, if any, exhibit free will? What distinguishes free will from will in general? Additional examples could be given of course to add to the (correct) impression that free will is a matter of degree and not always sharply distinguishable from movements of the mind that resemble it in some way.

I argue that free will is essentially a learned ability to exercise rational control over one's desires and volitions. There are four conditions that must be met to judge properly of any act that it is an act of free will in the full sense requisite for making those choices fit one for citizenship in the Kingdom of God: it must be intentional, uncoerced, voluntary, and autonomous.[4]

AN ACT OF FREE WILL MUST BE INTENTIONAL

To be an act of free will an act must be intentional. The category intentional has been the focus of most traditional discussions of the concept of free will. This is in part because the category of uncoerced has seemed to most thinkers obvious and uncomplicated, and because the category of voluntary has mistakenly been collapsed into the category of uncoerced. In general, people have been content with the conclusion that, if an act is not coerced by some external power and if it is intentional, it is an act of free will. This is unfortunate not only because it is mistaken but because it has led to the neglect of some very important ancillary considerations.

There is consensus, however, on the point that acts of free will must be intentional. For example, in the course of a hunting expedition I shoot and kill Jones even though I did not intend to do it; I stumbled over a hidden log and my gun accidentally discharged. This fact may provide me with an excuse so that I would not be held guilty of murder. I would be inclined to say in such a case that I did not will to do that, or it was not my doing. Therefore, we would say intention was lacking.

Intention is a conscious aiming at the attainment or the avoidance of some state of affairs. But we need now to unpack this very general notion, to see what it implies, to consider borderline cases, and to become aware of certain other conditions that must be present before such intention can occur.

Intending is a conscious state of mind, but it cannot be understood in isolation from that which is intended. It is an aiming at, and is therefore intrinsically related to some state of affairs beyond consciousness itself. The state of affairs that is beyond may itself be something internal to the life of the mind. That is, one may intend to curb or alter one's desires, one's moods, or even one's awareness. As we shall see, one ingredient in willing that is free, is the ability to exercise rational control over one's desires or to have the desire that one desires to have after reflection.

The relationship between intending and what is intended may be simple and direct, relatively simple and direct, or quite complicated. We may sing a song or play some recorded music because we get pleasure from hearing it. We may do a lot of research and work hard on the Manibucks Contract because we want a bonus, or because we want to buy a new sports car. We may invite the Smiths to our dinner party because they are good friends of the Joneses and because we want very much to get to know Mrs. Jones who is on the Board of Trustees of Topnotch College, where we hope our son, Johnny, will be accepted because his hope of going to Topnotch is the main thing that has motivated him to do well in school, which we consider to be very important, because ... and so on.

The relationship between intending and the states of affairs intended is well described by Duggan and Gert under the concept of incentives.[5] We have positive and negative desires, wanting or not wanting to obtain some state of affairs. These desires provide us with incentives to act or not to act in certain ways because we have developed a relevant set of beliefs about the world. Thus, we believe that doing, or bringing about, A will cause or increase the likelihood of B, or prevent or decrease the likelihood of B.

Feeling a desire does not produce the state of affairs that can satisfy the desire, nor the action that might lead to it. Aiming at is not mere desire but is desire that activates volition. Volition is willing, but the willing is blind (either merely instinctual or random) unless it is guided by knowledge (or belief). Knowledge (or belief) is a necessary condition for awareness of incentives. There can be an incentive for doing A, only if one believes that doing A will lead to the desired state of affairs. Willing that is blind cannot be free, because by free will we mean the ability to desire and to will as we want to on reflection; it is the ability to exercise rational control over our desires and volitions. Infants do not have the ability of free will because they do not have awareness of incentives on a fund of beliefs about how things are connected in the world. They have desires and volitions but they do not have as the basis for reflecting on whether these desires are the ones they truly want, or for adapting their desires and volitions in light of the consequences of their acting on the desires they happen to have.

In brief, the intentional component of willing consciously aims at the attainment or avoidance of some state of affairs. Again, with reference to the intentional component, what is necessary before the willing can be free is the ability to confirm or to adjust one's aim in the light of rational reflection on the incentives for acting and for not acting in a certain way. Such reflection can be rational only to the degree that the incentives are understood in the context of an appropriate body of reasonable beliefs about the way things are connected in the world.

Of course, our beliefs are sometimes mistaken. In the case of a will that is free the intending of X depends in part on beliefs about the way in which X is connected with other states of affairs, and upon the ability to adjust those beliefs in the light of further evidence. The fact that a certain volition is based in part upon a belief that is false does not of itself render that volition unfree (or irrational). It may be quite reasonable for a person, situated thus and so in history and belonging to such and such a culture, to believe something that turns out to be false. Evidence changes and accumulates, and along with that go changes in what is reasonable for a person to believe or to believe he or she knows. It would not be irrational for a fifteenth century priest to believe the moon is perfectly spherical in shape, or for a fifteenth century physician to believe bleeding will help a consumptive patient. Thus, the ability of free will is compatible with the holding of beliefs that are in fact false. But it is not compatible with the holding of beliefs that are in principle unchangeable—that are wholly unreformable no matter what evidence turns up. For example if Stern, a refugee from Nazi persecution, refuses to leave his house in Chicago because he has seen Krupp in the city and believes that Krupp is a Nazi who has come to kill him, we would not necessarily judge Stern irrational, or his decision is unfree. But if Stern persisted in those beliefs and decisions, in spite of much inconvenience to himself, and in spite of massive evidence that Krupp has been a mild and benign teller in the neighborhood bank for the past fifty years, we would begin to suspect Stern suffers from a compulsive obsession. If Stern is not able to exercise rational control over his desires and volitions, or, to put it another way, his will has been disabled and is not free.

I intend to do A, and do A in the belief that my action will bring about B, which I desire. With respect to the criterion of intention alone, my action exhibits free will so long as the beliefs integral to the intention are not irrational and impervious to further reflection in the light of new evidence. If I do A, and the consequence over several trials is not-B, something I do not desire, and I continue to do A, I would properly be judged irrational and not to possess free will as far as this particular behavioral scenario is concerned.

The first main point I want to make in connection with the topic of intention is: intention depends on learning, upon the formation of reasonable beliefs about the way things are connected in the world, and on the revisability of those beliefs upon reflection in the light of new evidence.

It is worth noting in passing that this sort of relationship between intention, belief, and knowledge is implied in the way in which we employ the notion of negligence, either in everyday life or in the law. Earlier, I used the example of a person who shot and killed someone by accident. That he did not intend what happened, I suggested, may provide him with an excuse.[6] But suppose that the hunter who killed Jones was an experienced hunter, who knew or should have known it is extremely dangerous to carry a loaded gun in open country without engaging the safety catch. In this case he may be properly charged, perhaps not with murder, but with negligent homicide. And are we not inclined to say that a person who has no experience or knowledge of guns ought not to go out on that sort of hunting expedition? There is an interesting implication of such common sense and legal judgments. Not only does the ability to have free will depend on the development of relevant beliefs and knowledge, but there is some sort of very general moral responsibility to become informed about the way the world goes.

Not all uncoerced actions of which I am conscious can be regarded as intentional; some obviously cannot, others obviously can, and there are borderline cases that are not clear. We might set these in a sort of continuum, of which there would be many more members than given here. The blinking of my right eye is clearly not intentional. I am acutely conscious of it and have tried everything I can think of to stop it, but I cannot. I have a tic. Clearly intentional is what I am doing right now, not simply poking my fingers randomly at the keys of this word processor, but trying to communicate to others just what is involved in doing something intentionally.

There are borderline cases; it is not always clear what we should say about habitual or spontaneous acts, and it is in connection with these acts that the claim arises that intending does not always involve deliberation. I put on my shoe, lace it up and tie it, as I do every morning. Did I intend to do this? Did I consciously aim at it? As I try to remember my state of consciousness as I did it, perhaps I am not quite sure. I'm inclined to say the actions were mere habit, but more and more, habitual actions resemble intentional ones as the actions becomes more complex. I get up on Sunday morning at 8:00 A.M., dress, go down to the corner news stand and buy the morning paper, bring it home and read it over breakfast, as I always do. "It is my habit," I say. But it would not be far-fetched to say that it was intentional as well, because in a longer and more complex sequence, it is almost inevitable that there would be at least moments of consciously thinking about what I am doing. And there is another reason, namely, that in complex and adaptive sequences, the series of acts were once intentional. On the first occasion, they were deliberately thought out, but decreasingly so with subsequent repetitions, until the routine became more habitual. But even so they do not become mere habit, which is clear on those occasions when the sequence is disturbed by unusual circumstances. For example, one Sunday morning a fierce blizzard is raging, so I do not go to the newsstand. The change in my routine on this occasion betrays none of the signs of the struggles that are involved in breaking a habit.

What about spontaneous actions? Do they exhibit intention? I see a person bleeding and writhing in pain on the pavement. I rush over and give help as best I can. Did I do this deliberately, or intentionally? Not deliberately, for I didn't think about it at all. I acted spontaneously. Can I say I intended to act as I did? I was not thinking about intention, and in retrospect, I might say, "Well, if I didn't do it intentionally, I certainly would have intended to do it if I had thought about it." But I was over there doing this and that, "before I knew it." This action has all the marks of spontaneity that characterize less momentous examples. Walking down the street one fine spring day, I toss my hat in the air and break into a song. If someone asked, "Why did you do that?" I might quite properly reply, "For no reason at all. I just felt like it." Perhaps Good Samaritans just feel like doing what she or he does.

Some theologians have supposed that the angels in heaven are so thoroughly imbued with infused grace that they naturally and spontaneously praise God. And the merit of the praise is not dimmed, but rather enhanced by its very spontaneity.

Although I do not deny that deliberation may be absent from a spontaneous act in the moment of action, such actions are bounded fore and aft by deliberation. We are not born Good Samaritans (or with any other complex pattern of behavior). The gradual shaping of character that would behave spontaneously in this way bespeaks a program of moral education, which was deliberate, either on the part of the agent in his or her earlier years, or on the part of such educators as parents.

Spontaneous actions are also bounded aft by deliberation. It may be useful to clarify this by criticizing a few points in the analysis given by H. Frankfurt, who maintains that deliberation is not necessarily involved in the shaping (or activity) of a will that is free.[7] Reference to Frankfurt's work has the added advantage that his basic concept of free will helps to make intuitively clear my view of free will as the ability to exercise rational control over one's desires and volitions. First, let us look at what he means by free will. Second, let us assess the point he makes about spontaneity and deliberation. What follows is a brief summary of the relevant portions of the article.

Animals, as well as humans, have desires. The lion desires the flesh of the gazelle. This is a first-order desire.[8] Not every first-order desire of an agent constitutes his will; one may have a number of competing desires, only one of which leads to action; or one may have a desire that does not lead to action. Will is *effective* first-order desire of the agent. The agent A exhibits will when "A's desire to do X is what is motivating A to do what he is actually doing."[9]

Frankfurt's interest is to connect the concept of free will with the concept of a person, and therefore, he asks what is distinctive about the willing of human beings. What is distinctive is "the capacity for reflective self-evaluation that is manifested in the formation of second-order desires."[10] A second-order desire is a desire to have, or not to have, a desire of the first-order. The Good Samaritan not only desires to help the victim, but on reflection desires to desire to help the victim. An addict desires a drug and may also desire to desire it; or he may desire not to desire it. If an agent does not care what desires shall move him to action, he is a wanton and, to that extent, not a person.[11] All animals and infants fall into this category. A wanton may be rational in the sense of being able to calculate how best to fulfill desire, but not in the sense of being able to control desires on the basis of reflection.

Second-order desire is not in itself sufficient to constitute free will. Frankfurt gives the example of a physician who has a drug addict under his care, and who desires to desire the drug the addict craves. The psychian wants to be able to feel what it is like to have that desire, but he does not want to become an addict. He does not want that desire to be effective. One may have a second-order desire that one does not want to become effective, or to constitute one's will. When one does on reflection want a second-order desire to become effective, one has a second-order volition.

We are now in a position to state Frankfurt's definition of free will, which clearly reflects my own contention that free will is the ability to exercise rational control over one's desires. He says: "freedom of the will means ... that he is free to will what he wants to will, or to have the will he wants ... securing the conformity of his will to his second-order volitions."[12] Freedom of the will is not the freedom to do whatever we want to do for there are sometimes obstacles beyond our control which prevent that outcome. Freedom of the will has to do, rather, with rational control over one's desires.

According to Frankfurt, the ability that is free will, is rooted in the capacity human beings have "of wanting to be different, in their preferences and purposes, from what they are. ... [This is] the capacity for reflective self-evaluation that is manifested in the formation of second-order desires."[13]

It is clear that this analysis supports the view I have been putting forward. But there are two points at which I feel obliged to criticize Frankfurt—points at which he suggests things that seem odd, or even mistaken, in the light of his own analysis.

On Frankfurt's account, free will depends on the capacity to form and is exhibited in the formation of at least second-order desires and volitions. Upon reflection one desires to desire the desire one has, or desires to have a different desire. On reflection, one wants to have the will that one has, or wants to have a different will. Frankfurt notes that a "person may have desires and volitions of a higher order than second."[14] That is, upon further reflection one may desire to desire to desire something other than what one now desires to desire (and *mutatis mutandis* regarding volitions).

I want to suggest, as Frankfurt does not, that the capacity that is free will in principle involves a capacity for indefinitely higher and higher orders of desires and volitions. Frankfurt mentions this possibility but gives it short shrift. His distaste for indefinite reflexivity springs obviously from practical concerns. If one always reflected further on whether one's desires and volitions were what one wanted, one would never reach the point of decision and action. It would be, Frankfurt says, "a case of humanization run wild."[15]

What Frankfurt advocates is that one cut off such an indefinite series of reflections by identifying oneself "decisively with one of his first order desires."[16] Failing to identify oneself decisively, one loses oneself in the realm of abstract possibilities. If one never reflects upon one's desires, but merely acts upon whichever desire is strongest at the moment, these one is a wanton, and for Frankfurt, this is a sub-human category. If one never stops the chain of reflection by decisive choice, the self is lost in the infinitude of possibility.

Having reflected upon one's desires, having willed a certain type of action in situations of such and such a sort, and having decisively chosen that action to be your characteristic will, situations of that sort may become more and more unthinking, more spontaneous. Such a development does not diminish the freedom of the will in any way. Such a person can aptly be described in the formula Frankfurt uses to characterize someone who acts with a will that is free: "he did what he wanted to do, did it because he wanted to do it, and the will that moved him was the will he wanted."[17] The case of spontaneous action requires only a slight amendment: the will that moved him was the will that had become such a settled part of his character he was no longer conscious of it, but one which he would consciously want, if he stopped to think about it, and which he is free to reconsider, if circumstances or evidence change.

What if there is a change in the situation and/or beliefs of the agent? Let us again imagine the scene described above and the action of the Good Samaritan, but with a few changes. The Good Samaritan sees someone bleeding and writhing in pain on the pavement. She starts to go to the side of the victim, but standing over the victim is a man with a club, and with him are three other men with guns. The man says, "Back off or we'll kill you," and she believes he means it. Well, perhaps our Good Samaritan is such a saint she cares nothing for her own safety. But suppose the threatening man is holding a hand grenade and says, "Back off or I'll throw this grenade into that group of children over there," and she believes that he surely under these altered circumstance our Good Samaritan *cannot without deliberation* simply act as she has habitually done, for such blind repitition would certainly not exhibit national control.

The will, which is expressed in such actions, is not fully free unless the agent has the capacity to reflect further, if and when a new situation or new evidence arises. Given the fact that novel situations arise, the person who has the ability that is free will must always be able to reflect on whether or not, here and now, in this situation and with these likely consequences, the habitual response is really the one wanted. Clearly, this sort of further reflection amounts to deliberation.

There is an additional reason for insisting free will involves deliberation. This reason emerges in the context of the discussion of the voluntary aspect of free will (see pp. 59–62).

AN ACT OF FREE WILL MUST BE UNCOERCED

To be an act of free will, an act must be uncoerced. Having been coerced to do X, an act otherwise blameworthy, may provide an excuse for having done X. I should not be held guilty of detonating the bomb in the supermarket, even if my fingerprints were found on the detonator, if I could prove that someone stronger than I forced my finger to press the button. An action of a person who is coerced is really not his own; he is not an agent, or as Aristotle put it, "nothing is contributed by the person who is acting or feeling the passion, e.g. if he were to be carried somewhere by a wind, or by men who had him in their power."[18]

For the most part, the tradition in both philosophy and theology has followed Aristotle in the view that an act of free will is adequately described as intentional and uncoerced. In the case of coercion, the spring of action is outside the person; in the case of intention it is inside the person.

The category of voluntary has not been thought to be required, for it seemed obvious to those in this tradition that an intentional, uncoerced action is by definition voluntary. But this is a mistake,—a mistake that leads to confusion on some points highly relevant to our inquiry. Incidentally, Aristotle was aware that the two categories, intentional and uncoerced, were not adequate to deal with all cases. In the *Nicomachean Ethics* he discusses mixed cases (i.e. cases in which coerced actions nevertheless seem to be voluntary).[19] But Aristotle does not pursue the matter.

We think of coercion as being forced to do something against (or at least without) our will and, therefore, as something for which we ourselves are not responsible. This notion is deeply imbedded both in common sense and in law. In fact, all of this has seemed so obvious, little attention has been paid to issues raised by borderline cases, or to the question of whether or not coercion may arise due to factors other than external physical force. Paying heed to these factors is crucial if we want more than a vague concept of free will.

We know of cases in which it is difficult to be certain, in judging the action of another, whether or not that person was coerced. Did the prisoner of war give away vital secrets to the enemy under torture? How bad was the torture? But we would do well to note that it is sometimes difficult to arrive at a proper judgment in these matters even with regard to oneself. As Freud demonstrates, we are not always aware of the deepest springs of our own actions.

There are kinds of action, undoubtedly actuated by deep psychological or physiological forces that are beyond the conscious control of the agent, and are worthy of special note at this point. A person suffering from a compulsive neurosis cannot control certain of his or her actions. The kleptomaniac cannot help stealing. A person suffering from a certain phobia cannot control his or her feelings in certain situations, and these feelings may become strong enough to compel the person to act in a certain way, or to render the person incapable of acting in a certain way. The addict feels compelled to inject the heroin, or to steal to get the money to buy the heroin.

Should we treat such actions as being coerced? In this case, we have to speak of two types of coercion: by forces outside the agent and by internal forces. This way of thinking may seem quite plausible but has one big drawback. It obscures one very important distinction between the two sub-categories. In cases where the agent is physically forced by an external power to do X, physical force is needed precisely because the agent does not will to do X. The agent's body is unfree, but not his will. In cases of psychological compulsion, phobias, or addictions it seems the will itself is unfree, or divided and incapable of willing not to do X. There seems to be some sort of "disability of the will."[20] In order to keep this distinction clearly in mind, actions of this sort are not treated as examples of coercion but as unvoluntary acts.[21] This distinction is of considerable importance in assessing the cogency of various forms of the free will defense. In at least one major Christian theological tradition, the will of post-adamic humans has been described in such a way as to render at least plausible the conclusion that post-adamic humans suffer from a disability of the will and, therefore, they do not sin voluntarily.

Freely willing to do X, as noted earlier, involves intention, and intention involves responding to incentives, which in turn involve beliefs about the way things are connected in the world. Incentives may become so strong as to be coercive. The promise of $5 for doing X functions as an incentive for doing X; so would the promise of $1,000,000. Now, we may or may not regard such a promise as coercive. We may say not only that the agent should resist that promise but that he can. But surely incentives vary in degree in such a way there will be borderline cases, and in such a way some incentives become coercive. You are ordered to push the button that will detonate the bomb in the supermarket. You firmly refuse. You are again ordered to do so under a threat: "Do it, or I'll kill your wife!" or "Do it, or I'll kill you!" We can imagine the stakes being escalated further and further. The point here is simply that what functions as an incentive, and how strong that incentive is, depends upon one's beliefs as well as one's feelings and desires. One does or does not believe the button is the detonator of a large bomb, that the bomb is located in a busy supermarket (one believes it is in an empty field). One believes that the threatening thug means to carry out his treat, or does not. One's feelings and desires are also obviously relevant. Perhaps one hates one's wife, or is tired of living.

AN ACT OF FREE WILL MUST BE VOLUNTARY

In order to be an act of free will an act must be voluntary. It has seemed to many that an action is freely willed so long as it is not coerced and is intentionally chosen. It is as though freedom of the will were palpably evident, at least to ourselves, in the choosing and doing. Thus, Augustine observes: "If we cannot will without willing, those who will have will. Our will would not be will unless it were in our power. Because it is in our power, it is free."[22] Again, he says:

> There is nothing so much in our power as is the will itself. For as soon as we will, immediately will is there. We can say rightly that we do not die voluntarily but from necessity. But who but a raving fool would say that it is not voluntary that we will?[23]

Indeed, this view has become established in the tradition. As noted earlier, it has been held that if an act is intentional and uncoerced it is also voluntary and an act of free will. Voluntary has been treated as an equivalent of uncoerced. This view, however, in spite of its prestige, is mistaken; moreover, failure to note why it is mistaken has led to some misconceptions about the nature of free will—misconceptions that are directly related to certain inadequacies in the way in which the free will defense has been formulated. An act may be both intentional and uncoerced and yet not be an act of free will.

A person may will something intentionally under no coercion and yet not do so with free will. A person can will something and yet lack the ability to will things of that sort. To put it in another way, a person may will something while suffering from a disability of the will. This, of course, seems highly paradoxical. The following analogy may help make the notion seem less odd. It is quite possible for a person to do something intentionally even though he lacks the ability to do something of that sort. On a golfing outing I sink a 100-yard putt. I intended to do that. That's what I had in mind and hoped for as I made the stroke. Yet, when my abilities as a golfer are objectively assessed, no one would say, "He has the ability to sink 100-yard putts!" It was sheer luck. The force of this analogy will come out when we consider persons who suffer from certain disabilities of the will, which make them unable to do things of a certain sort in general, even though on some particular occasion they may do an act of that sort.

Free will implies the ability to will to do things of a certain sort and the ability to refrain from doing them under appropriate circumstances. We must include both of these abilities if we are to understand the crucial difference between normal people and those who suffer from disabilities of the will. Compulsives, phobics, and addicts frequently exhibit this sort of disability. We would not say of the kleptomaniac, who frequently and intentionally wills to steal jewelry from the store, that in doing so he or she exhibits free will unless he or she also exhibits the ability to refrain from stealing jewelry. This would be so, even if, on some one or few particular occasions, he or she refrained from stealing because of the belief that the jewelry was in fact a cleverly disguised bomb. The person suffering from claustrophobia does not have the ability to will to enter small, enclosed spaces, even if on one or several occasions he or she does so. Someone has said, "Get in the trunk of that car, or I'll blow your brains out." The heroin addict does not have the ability to will not to inject heroin, even if on some occasion he or she refrains, firmly believing that an enemy has laced the heroin with cyanide. The delusional person may not be able to will to do certain things because he or she cannot be persuaded by any amount of evidence to change a belief, which implies that doing that sort of thing would be extremely dangerous. In short, the person who wills to do something may not, in spite of all outward appearances, be willing to do that thing freely, but may be driven by fears, needs, or beliefs entirely beyond his or her control. Examples of such internal states are not examples of ordinary coercion, and it leads to confusion if one simply puts down such states as instances of internal coercion. What is decisive in the case of unvoluntary actions is not merely there is a coercive force (either external or internal) but that the agent lacks rational control over how she or he will respond to coercive force. In the case of unvoluntary actions the will itself has somehow become disabled and the response is triggered by some sort of irrational and uncontrollable mental state.[24]

Recall earlier comments on further reflection (pp. 56–57). I, the heroin addict, may will to inject heroin, but I do not will with a will that is free, unless I also have the capacity to will not to inject the heroin. I must be able to reflect further upon the action I contemplate doing and must be able, under appropriate circumstances, to decide that that will is not the will I want. The addict, or claustrophobic, is able to refrain from doing what she or he habitually does only when coerced, and whatever is done under coercion is not free.

Since I make use of Frankfurt's concept of free will, I would also like to mention what is to me a needlessly confusing passage in the article I cited—a confusion that is easily cleared up when one recognizes that actions must be voluntary, intentional, and uncoerced if they are to exhibit freedom of the will. Frankfurt says that one can "act of one's own free will and yet not have a will that is free."[25] He interprets the phrase "of his own free will" to mean "he did what he wanted to do, did it because he wanted to do it, and the will that moved him was the will he wanted."[26] This sounds at first like a will that is as free as anyone might want, but what is missing is the ability of the agent to reflect further (and decide accordingly) as to whether or not this will that he wants is really the will that he wants. This judgment is implicit in Frankfurt's own observation: "his will is outside his control."[27] It is not just a coincidence that the example of such a person that he (Frankfurt) gives is an addict, in this case a willing addict. Such a person, Frankfurt supposes, suffers "the overdetermination of his first-order desire" due to the fact that he is physiologically addicted.[28] But to speak of a person doing something of his own free will even though he did not have a will that was free is confusing. The confusion is typical of many that arise from the failure to acknowledge the category of voluntary as essential to freedom of the will. With that category at our disposal, we should say of such an individual that he did not act of his own free will because his action was unvoluntary; he suffered from a disability of the will, which is precisely what is implied by Frankfurt's own characterization: "his will is outside his control."

A voluntary act is one that we are free to perform and also free to refrain from performing. As in connection with our consideration of intentionality, the question of deliberation arises here as well. No doubt most voluntary acts, especially those that have become habitual, occur without conscious deliberation in the moment of decision. This is analogous to cases of spontaneous intentional acts. If our volitions are truly free, we exercise the ability to reconsider even those that have become habitual, when new circumstances or evidence warrants.

AN ACT OF FREE WILL MUST BE AUTONOMOUS

As noted, free will is a complex set of abilities, depends on a complex set of conditions, and is a matter of degree. The most fully developed free will, in the sense requisite for citizenship in the Kingdom of God, is also autonomous.

In chapter 3, we noted that Mackie and Flew, on the one hand, and Plantinga, on the other, were assuming different definitions of free will. Plantinga clearly assumes free will implies autonomy though he does not explicate this concept in detail. Plantinga is content to characterize autonomy in negative terms: an action that exhibits free will is such, he says, that "no antecedent conditions and/or causal laws determine that he will perform that action, or that he won't."[29] This definition is negative because it depends on the view that what is involved in an act of free will, or an autonomous act, can be made clear simply be saying that it is not determined. This is most unfortunate for at least two reasons. First, the issue between determinism and indeterminism can not be settled. Second, this notion of an act of free will as an undetermined act lends force to the cogent attack that many philosophers have made on the position of those advocates of free will who depend upon the doctrine of indeterminism. If an act is simply undetermined it is not only unpredictable (which, of course, is what the traditional free willers want to stress), it would also be arbitrarily and unaccountably related to the character of the agent. For example, one would have no basis for judging John a reliably honest person, for on the next pertinent occasion John might just decide to cheat or steal.

Yet we have an intuitive notion of what we mean by autonomy. When we say a person's act is autonomous, we mean that no force, or combination of forces, outside of his own volition in the moment of his choice, is sufficient to make him act in just that way. What I want to note, and explore further, however, is that this common sense notion in no way denies there are antecedent conditions which are necessary to an action, if that action is an act of free will. Nor does it deny that the sum of these necessary antecedent conditions may make a certain kind of action more probable. In the theological context, which is relevant to our inquiry, the notion of autonomy means that an act of free will that is autonomous cannot logically have God's will alone as its sufficient cause. If we are free and autonomous persons, to that extent and in those situations in which we instantiate that autonomy, our behavior cannot simply be caused by God or built into us by a regimen of divine conditioning.

The negative aspect of an autonomous act, then, can be simply stated: antecedent causes outside the volition of the agent in the moment of decision are not sufficient to account for the act. A more positive and detailed explication of the concept is more difficult, because it is hard to leave behind the habit of thinking in terms of a dichotomy between causal determinism and indeterminism. The view that I suggest will no doubt be regarded as a form of indeterminism, but it is one that does not simply rely on the negative judgment that acts of free will are not completely determined. I articulate this view in more detail in chapter 8.

I maintain that the concept of free will developed in this chapter is more complete and more adequate than the one that has dominated traditional formulations of the free will defense. In the next chapter I indicate how it leads to a modification of the free will defense and how this modification formulation strengthens the free will defense. In addition, in chapter 8, I describe more fully what constitutes the best available concept of free will. I defer that description until chapter 8 because it makes sense in the context of the process view, which I set forth there.

Chapter 7

A Revised Free Will Defense

In this chapter I want first to state very succinctly the free will defense in its optimal form. Second, I want to elaborate and comment on a few of its chief elements. Third, I want to suggest ways in which it helps to meet some of the more serious problems, which arise for the more traditional formulation. Most changes from the traditional formulation of the free will defense, arise from analysis of the concept of free will discussed in chapter 6.

THE REVISED FREE WILL DEFENSE

Since the very nature of God is love, he brings into being creatures[1] whom he can love and who can respond in love for God. Indeed, the purpose and goal of creation is determined by this essential nature of God: to bring about a Kingdom of God, defined as a community in which God and his creatures freely love one another and where all creatures themselves are bound together in mutual love and justice. Loving that is not chosen with a will that is free is not genuine love. God's purpose and goal, when attained, would constitute the highest possible good for all creatures. It would be a good so great as to compensate for any and all evils that might be either necessary to its attainment or unavoidable in attaining it. As we have seen, given God's decision to create a world suitable for learning the abilities of free will, it is necessary that there be some natural evils though no particular natural evil is necessary. Moreover, given free will and the need to learn the abilities of free will, no particular instance of moral evil could have been avoided by divine fiat, and some moral evils must exist for creatures to learn from the consequences of choosing either good or evil to make rational choice of the good.

Love between creatures, or between creatures and God, is genuine and of the highest value only when it is freely given by an autonomous moral agent, and virtues essential to justice are genuine only when freely chosen. For this reason, God made creatures of such a sort that they would be capable both of learning abilities that constitute moral free will, and choosing to shape their behavior in keeping with the virtues of love and justice. God does not simply give these abilities to his creatures, or create them with these abilities from the outset, for this is incompatible with being autonomous. These abilities must be acquired (if they are acquired) through the free and rational choices of the creatures, and in the context of considerable knowledge about the way things work in the world. In order for creatures to learn that there are moral choices to be made, and to learn to make them rightly, the world must necessarily include natural evils; for no choice would ever be morally significant if, no matter what were chosen, there were no evil consequences such as pain or death. Moreover, if creatures are to learn to make morally proper choices in accordance with virtues of love and justice, and to make them of their own free will, they must learn by experience the consequences of making such choices, as well as the consequences of making morally wrong choices. Therefore, such creatures must live in a world where there are moral evils as well as natural evils. Since their choices are to be free, it is not logically possible for anyone, even God, to prevent immoral choices. Moral evils are thus both necessary and unavoidable. Knowing that his great goal required a world in which both natural and moral evils would arise, God nevertheless deemed it good to create such a world. For a world in which there is the possibility of the Kingdom of God, even at the cost of the sorts of evils mentioned, is better than no world, and therefore no love,[2] or a world in which God guarantees that there will be no evil, and therefore no free will. In terms of human existence, a life that includes the possibility of attaining free will and the virtues of the Kingdom of God, even though necessarily at the cost of suffering, is better than the life of an automaton which is incapable of suffering but also incapable of love. This is a basic value judgment which is implicit or explicit in Christian theology.

THE BASIC VALUE JUDGMENT

From Augustine onwards, major theologians of the tradition have affirmed that the cogency of the free will defense depends among other things upon the above value judgment. The judgment itself seems reasonable. Some suggest that a world without any evil at all would be better, but they do not explicitly compare a world without evil and without free will to a world with free will and those evils that are either necessary or unavoidable.

How does one justify a basic value judgment? When we understand what this justification involves, we will see why it is unreasonable to predict that there will ever be universal agreement on the cogency of even an optimally formulated free will defense. For there is finally no way reason can decide between two basic value judgments.

The situation is somewhat different in the case of relative or conditional value judgments. A is a good way to produce X. B is a better way to produce X, meaning that it is more likely than A to produce X. C is a poor way to produce X. If you do D, you'll never produce X. In such cases the value in question (i.e. of A, B, C, or D) is ascertainable on the basis of its tendency to either produce or preclude certain results. We can make such judgments, and justify them, to the extent that we can accumulate the relevant empirical data. But it is easy to see that the absolute value of any of these antecedents depends on the value of the results one is aiming at.

When we ask about basic value judgments, we want to know about the intrinsic value of something—or to put it another way, we want to know if that something is good in and of itself and not merely as a means to some other end. Of course, the situation is rather more complex, for in the actual world there is no something that is unrelated to other things, whose existence is devoid of further consequences. We should make our basic value judgments by judging their intrinsic value as described above (i.e. as ends in themselves) but with the understanding such judgments are revisable in the light of further relevant information. Incidentally, this is analogous to the way in which our reflections on what we really desire are open to revision in the light of further information (see pp. 56–57). We order our hierarchy of instrumental values in the light of our judgment that X is intrinsically valuable as an end in itself. If we were to learn through experience that the attainment of X in fact has consequences, or necessary antecedents, which we had not foreseen and which we judge to be sufficiently evil, we should revise our basic value judgment regarding X.

With this proviso in mind, it is still the case, however, that our valuation of something must finally come to a conclusion in a judgment for which we can give no further justification than the capacity of that something to elicit approval from us and from any who might ask why it is a basic value. Humans, insofar as they are rational, want to know why they should do this and why they should not do that. The explanations as to why finally peter out in a basic value judgment. Perhaps the following example of the process will help to make the point clearer. I make the moral judgment that it is wrong to deceive (or to tell a lie). Someone asks why it's wrong. I reply that if you (or I) tell lies, these will likely and eventually be discovered, and I will no longer trust you (or you me). I add that, if I accord myself the privilege of deceiving, I implicitly grant that same right to you, because I have to acknowledge that it would be irrational of you to be bound by a rule of truth telling when I am not. This would place you at a disadvantage in every transaction between the two of us. Someone asks what would be so bad about a breakdown of mutual trust between people. I say that this would be bad because it would discourage any cooperative ventures between people. And someone asks why it would be bad if there were no cooperative ventures. I reply that, if there were no cooperative ventures, humans would not be able to be as productive as they are in providing the necessities of life, or as successful in fending off natural forces which threaten them. Someone asks why it would be bad if our production of the necessities of life were very meager. I reply that this would lead, among other things, to people becoming cold and hungry. Someone asks what would be wrong with that. I reply that being cold and being hungry is very painful. Someone asks what is wrong with pain. At this point, we have reached the end of the offering of reasons and justifications. One might reply that it just is the case that suffering pain is evil.[3] Or perhaps one might illustrate one's point by whacking the questioner's knuckles very hard with a hickory rod. At this point one has reached a basic value judgment.

The same sort of thing can be said of positive basic value judgments. The whole enterprise of Christian theodicy depends upon the judgment that the very highest good for humans is living together in a relationship of freely given (and received) love. The Christian is taught to understand what is involved in such love by contemplating the life and teachings of Jesus, who is regarded as the fullest manifestation of the nature and will of God. If someone were to ask why this is good, one would finally and simply have to describe what that sort of relationship involves and to appeal to the other to see that it is the greatest possible good.

THE NECESSITY AND UNAVOIDABILITY OF EVIL

My revision of the free will defense provides a fuller and more detailed understanding of why it is necessary (if free will is to be developed), that there be a process of learning that includes experiences of actual moral and natural evils. Such a process is implied by Origen's declaration that "He gave us free will that the virtues we acquire might be our own."[4] It is even more clearly implied by Irenaeus's notion that we must ourselves grow up into the likeness of God. And it is clearly set forth in John Hick's "soul-making theodicy"[5] Yet none of these show in detail how the very nature of free will itself requires such a development. This is not surprising in view of another defect in traditional formulations of the free will defense: namely, failure to provide an adequate analysis of the concept of free will and the conditions necessary to its development.

Showing that the necessity for evils is implied in the very concept of free will also helps to strengthen some of the specific lines of argument typical of traditional theodicies. Consider, for example, the influential contrast theory of Augustine. In spite of its intuitive appeal, the argument doesn't quite work as he puts it. For it is not the case that in general we are able to appreciate goods only by way of contrast with evils. It is, however, the case that in order to learn to make a rational and autonomous choice which is morally significant, we must experience actual evils and their consequences, as well as actual goods and their consequences.

I suggest that my formulation of the free will defense provides a better line of argument and that it is persuasive if one grants the basic value judgment, which lies at its foundation. This judgment places a virtually incommensurate value on the development of virtues which are freely chosen by the autonomous moral will of those persons who are fit to become citizens of the Kingdom of God. The suggestion is that God has created and is justified in creating a world in which such development is possible, in spite of the fact that such a world necessarily includes natural and moral evils.

BUT WHY SO MUCH EVIL?

If my reformulation of the free will defense makes it a stronger support for Christian theodicy, it still does not remove all questions and problems. I strive to keep the discussion and the arguments within the parameters of the dominant mainline theology of the Christian tradition,[6] but given that type of theodicy, it is very difficult, if not impossible, to give a satisfactory answer to the question of why there should be so much evil. If my reformulation is valid, then we can see why some natural and moral evils are necessary, given the great goal of God. But the mainline tradition insists upon a high conception of the omnipotence, omniscience, and perfect goodness of God. The common view is that God's omnipotence implies that he can do anything whatsoever that is conceivable without logical contradiction. The problem that arises is why the omnipotent God could not have created a world and human beings in such a way that there would be the evils requisite to the process of learning the abilities of free will, but such that there would be far fewer and less grievous evils—with evils, as it were, defined by strict boundaries and under better control.

In considering possible orthodox responses to this problem, the difference between moral and natural evils becomes important. There is an intuitive plausibility to the argument, often advanced in the mainline tradition, that if human beings have free will, even the omnipotent God cannot limit the amount or gravity of moral evils, that is, the evils due to human misuse of free will. To say that God enforces such limits and that the human will is free would constitute a logical contradiction. But I think that this response is not wholly adequate when one considers other possibilities surely available to divine omnipotence without negating free will. For examples, humans could have been created by divine omnipotence with keener practical, moral intelligence, and better character. Equipped with keener intelligence, humans would not need instruction as to the moral imperatives. Alternatively, humane would be better able to follow the logic of the arguments that justify the moral imperatives. All would understand quite clearly why our practical reason demands that we behave morally. And humans could have been created with stronger and better character—not in such a way that they would feel no inclination to do what is wrong, or in such a way as never to do what is wrong, for if that were the case, then the experience of actual moral evils requisite to the learning and development of free will in its fullest form would be absent. But divine omnipotence might have made them with considerable increments of sympathy and might have placed them in an environment sufficiently less threatening as to result in a reduction of anxiety for self and one's self-interest. In short, God could have reduced the hostile, aggressive, vengeful inclinations of humans without absolutely eliminating them, and surely this would have resulted in a world containing less moral evil. As it is in the actual world, evil is rampant. The evils due to human wrongdoing are devilishly grievous and far beyond any measure of what is required for the learning of the abilities of moral free will.

When we consider natural evils, mainline or orthodox theodicies seem even more open to criticism. As we have noted, no choice would exhibit moral free will unless the world contained some natural evils. If there were no instances of pain, suffering, or death then no action one might choose would cause harm to another. Moral free will implies rational control over one's desires and volitions, that is, requires that one's choice depend upon an understanding of the connection between the contemplated action and the goods or evils likely to flow from it. We are not born with that understanding but must acquire it through experience of actual goods and evils. It is surely not necessary that natural evils be so many and so grievous as they are in the actual world. This judgment has been criticized by those who hold what I have called the super heroic view of the Christian life, a view which I described and questioned earlier (pp. 13–14).

Chapter 8

An Ecological Theology

In this final, rather speculative chapter, I suggest a somewhat more radical concept of the limitation of God's power. As we have seen, problems remain even for a revised and more adequate formulation of the free will defense. These are most problematical in connection with the problem of natural evil, but also troublesome in connection with the problem of moral evil. Given the traditional notion of God's omnipotence, it seems pretty clear that God, so conceived, could have achieved his great goal, the Kingdom of God, in a world he arranged so there would be fewer and less grievous evils.

There have, of course, been a number of thinkers who have commended the notion of a limited God.[1] These efforts have as a rule been greeted with scorn and derision. They seem to critics to be little more than *ad hoc*, desperate efforts to bolster the enterprise of theodicy and also to be heretical from a Christian standpoint. Be that as it may, I develop a notion, though helpful in relation to the problems I have mentioned, that has a much broader application in Christian theology and is not conjured up *ad hoc*, but is rather an integral part of a consistent and plausible metaphysical system.

In this chapter I articulate a revised concept of the divine power, as well as other revisions having to do with the whole notion of God's relation to the created world. These revisions would, if I am correct, mitigate and perhaps even solve, the remaining problems to which I have alluded.

I have used the term speculative to refer to the ideas I am about to develop. There are suggestions of the direction I want to take in the biblical texts, but a more complete notion of the revisions I have in mind depends on what I call an ecological theology. In beginning to develop this, I have been influenced by recent writings in the field of ecology and the field of evolutionary theory.[2] Perhaps even more influential has been the so-called process theology, which owes its initial inspiration to the work of Alfred North Whitehead and has been developed, in a way that seems most impressive, in the works of Charles Hartshorne.

This chapter is not only speculative but quite incomplete; it is really a sketch of issues to be considered in future work. The writings of Whitehead are difficult, intricate, and dependent on a wide variety of developments in what might be called the philosophy of science. To articulate and defend these ideas adequately would require a very lengthy treatise. In these respects, the writings of Hartshorne are more accessible, but still difficult. But my main reason for considering all of this to be speculative is that I have not firmly decided to what extent and in which particulars these process theology views are worthy of endorsement. For example, some of Whitehead's views regarding God, views in which Whitehead feels justified by his general metaphysical system, depart needlessly from more traditional concepts.

In spite of these reservations, I want to commend serious consideration of the revisions in theology that arise from an ecological understanding of God's relation to the created world.

BIBLICAL HINTS

The writer of Genesis tells us, after mentioning all of the particular things that were created, "And God saw everything that he had made, and behold, it was very good."[3] Suppose we underscore that everything in a way which, unfortunately, has not always been done in the tradition. Suppose we take the view that the goodness of anything is intimately related to the goodness of everything. Let us remember the way in which the text in Isaiah includes nature in the celebration of the culmination of God's great purpose. "The wolf and the lamb shall feed together, the lion shall eat straw like the ox; and dust shall be the serpent's food. They shall not hurt or destroy in all my holy mountain."[4] Or again, "For you shall go out in joy, and be led forth in peace; the mountains and the hills before you shall break forth into singing, and all the trees of the field shall clap their hands."[5]

Suppose we take a cosmically ecological view. According to the Gospel of John, "In the beginning was the Word, and the Word was with God and the Word was God. He was in the beginning with God; and all things were made through him, and without him was not anything made that was made."[6]

St. Paul sees an intimate interrelation of everything in the cosmos, not now as things are in the fallen world, but in the intention and purpose of God. "We know that the whole creation has been groaning in travail until now … as we wait for adoption as sons. …"[7]

Even more clearly is the ecological notion expressed in the following:

> He (Christ) is the image of the invisible God, the first-born of all creation; for in him all things were created, in heaven and on earth, visible and invisible … all things were created through him and for him. He is before all things, and in him all things hold together.[8]

The work of Christ in reconciling us to God[9] is at the same time reconciling all things to himself and to God. But this also implies that all things need to be reconciled. In the great cosmic drama of creation, the fall, and redemption all things are bound together.

NEW PERSPECTIVES

There is ample evidence from the history of almost any realm of thought, including the history of Christian thought, that changes in important aspects of a culture are accompanied by changes in that realm of thought. Some ideas are challenged and changed due to contact or conflict with a foreign culture. Some ideas appear to be impractical or false in the light of further experience. The notion of the covenant between Israel and Yahweh underwent significant changes under the influence of the great prophets of the Hebrew Bible—for example, the idea of a partiality for the nation of Israel quite independent of her ethical deportment being cast aside in favor of a universal ethical monotheism.

The traditional notion of divine omnipotence fits well with certain older cultural conceptions, which conceived of the proper arrangement of political power in a very hierarchical and absolutist way. The power of the king was once regarded as the highest power (on earth), and the power of the king was thought to be perfect when it was absolute. A king ruled by divine right, and one can understand how and why a king could believe l'état, c'est moi.

With the advance of democracy, exaltation of absolute power in the political realm has been repudiated and destroyed. Absolute power is not perfect power. In spite of this, one must admit that in many cultures (such as the United States) the greatest possible power is the object of great adulation. Superman is super. The extremely macho Rambo became a top box office attraction in the nation's movie houses, and his films are repeated ad nauseam on TV. In one film, Rambo defies and defeats well-armed Viet Cong. In another film he defeats red-necked, power-obsessed, and fascistic law enforcement officers.

Nevertheless, new perspectives have become influential, and at least two of these may prepare us to consider a revision of our thinking about the power of God. Hartshorne's point is, persuasive: namely, with regard to any attribute of God, we should think of it in terms of perfection.[10] The new perspectives I refer to insists that all power is not perfect, but is despotical.

One perspective I have in mind is feminist theology. Among the many contributions this movement has made to contemporary theology is its critique of the exclusively male and absolutely omnipotent God. God's power has been thought of as unlimited (except perhaps not extending to the ability to do things logically contradictory) and, quite often, completely arbitrary, so far as we can see. St. Paul, in explaining why God had hardened the heart of Pharaoh, indicates that God had hardened Pharaoh's heart for the purpose of showing his (God's) power. And when asked why God hardens one and shows his grace to another, St. Paul's answer is: "So then he has mercy upon whomever he wills, and he hardens the heart of whomever he wills."[11] St. Paul goes on to say, "You will say to me then, Why does he still find fault? For who can resist his will? But who are you, a man, to answer back to God?"[12] This repudiation of the right to a reason or rationale, is used by many theologians, who often cite these passages. Calvin makes clear that the whole concept of our relationship to God implies "before God we are less than the beasts."[13]

We might also recall the way Job is treated by God. According to the book of Job, Job demands an explanation for his unjustified suffering but the demand is never honored. Instead he is bludgeoned into abject submission by God's boastful recital of his great powers and, by contrast, Job's nothingness.

The tradition has often portrayed God as one who wants and wills humans to remain in ignorance, helplessness, and slavery to his own majestic all power. As one feminist writer puts it:

> An even more fundamental critique of classical theism has been produced by feminist critics who find in the classical conception of God a

not-too-subtle mask of an authoritarian patriarch, a "Father Knows Best" who, although removed from the world, controls it according to plan and keeps humans in a state of infantile subjection.[14]

To the feminist theologians, this is inconsistent with the notion that God is a God of love. Perhaps the most familiar metaphor for God that one finds in the Bible is of a loving father.[15] It is, of course, a metaphor taken from familiar human experience, and we have good reason to believe it is intended to point to a truth about God. And what a truly loving parent wants for his or her children is not that they remain perpetual infants, helpless and utterly dependent upon the superior power of a willful and arbitrary parent, but rather that they grow up, become mature and independent, as Dietrich Bonhoeffer implies in his *Letters and Papers from Prison*.[16]

Another perspective is that of ecology, a field of concern and study that is rather recent. When I studied Darwin's writings years ago, the concept of survival of the fittest was understood by me, and by many, as really meaning the survival of the strongest. We understood nature to be red in tooth and claw. The future belonged to the most powerful. Social Darwinism was used to justify ruthless competition in the market place. The destruction of economic enterprises that could not compete was regarded as a good thing—comparable to the way nature in weeding out unfit species. All of this is, of course, another illustration of the influence of the cultural views of a particular (and passing) historical setting.

Those influenced by the field of ecology see things quite differently and have transformed our (or at least my) reading of Darwin. When Darwin writes of the survival of the fittest his emphasis quite clearly is on the capacity of a given species to relate fittingly to the entire environment (physical and biological) in a way that is mutually supportive.[17]

I want now to support and extend these hints by sketching a broad metaphysical point of view, not including every aspect that usually enters into a metaphysical system, but emphasizing those that are relevant to the development of an ecological theology.

THE METAPHYSICAL CONTEXT

The world view, or metaphysical system, that seems suggestive of an ecological theology is called process philosophy or organismic philosophy. It owes its beginnings to the work of Alfred North Whitehead. Whitehead's most systematic treatise on the subject is *Process and Reality*.[18] I want to sketch the features of this metaphysic that are most relevant to the issues we are considering.

Process philosophy is extremely extensive, for, as Whitehead insists a metaphysical system must in principle account at least in a general way for every kind of event or entity. Whitehead invents new and unfamiliar terms to refer to many of his key concepts. Though I will (as far as I can remain faithful to Whitehead's ideas), depart from them at certain points. On some issues the writings of Charles Hartshorne, one of Whitehead's most influential followers, are clearer, and in Hartshorne, the theological implications are as a rule drawn out more fully and clearly than is the case with Whitehead himself. In more recent times, David Ray Griffen has written several astute and helpful works articulating the process theology point of view on the issues that concern us here.[19] In his distinguished career, Whitehead devoted himself primarily to issues of mathematics, logic, and science. It was quite late in his life that he turned to issues of religion in a systematic and serious way.

The relevance of process philosophy to an ecological theology can be stated rather briefly and clearly. Process philosophy builds on insights of quantum mechanics, field theory, and subatomic research in physics. As a result of these scientific advances, it now seems clear that the world (reality) is not made up of discrete and self-contained things located in absolute space and time. What exist at the most fundamental level are events, happenings, energy transactions, and processes. Moreover, modern field theory has made it clear that these energy events are not isolated from one another; on the contrary, given enough time, every energy event in the universe affects every other energy event (except those that occur simultaneously). What happens in what we call the here and now depends upon countless zillions of happenings in the past, and will affect countless zillions of happenings in the future.

It is no doubt difficult to imagine the sort of creative interaction and sensitive responsiveness in all events, even in those at the atomic and subatomic level, or to imagine that this immense organismic reality is lured towards ever greater mutual awareness and harmony. The difficulty in great part is due to the fact we see so much that runs counter to such an upward thrust. Yet, somehow in the midst of the destructive forces such complexity, mutuality, and sensitivity have in fact arisen, even to the level of consciousness and awareness of the long process that has led hither.

Perhaps such awareness is less difficult for a poetic imagination like that of Walt Whitman.

Rise after rise bow the phantoms behind me,
Afar down I see the huge first Nothing, I know I was even there,
I waited unseen and always, and slept through the lethargic mist,
And took my time, and took no hurt from the fetid carbon.
Long I was hugged close—long and long.
Immense have been the preparations for me,
Faithful and friendly the arms that have help'd me.
Cycles ferried my cradle, rowing and rowing like cheerful Boatmen,
For room to me stars kept aside in their own rings,
They sent influences to look after what was to hold me.
Before I was born out of my mother generations guided me,
My embryo has never been torpid, nothing could overlay it.
For it the nebula cohered to an orb,
The long slow strata piled to rest it on,
Vast vegetables gave it sustenance,
Monstrous sauroids transported it in their mouths and deposited it
    with care.
All forces have been steadily employ'd to complete and delight me.
Now on this spot I stand with my robust soul."[20]

Another important aspect of process thought has to do with the concept of free will, which is central to the free will defense and has not been adequately formulated in the tradition. I argued earlier that it is not necessary to settle the debate between the determinists and the indeterminists in order to clarify the concept of free will; and that, I maintain, is the case. It is interesting, though, that in process philosophy a concept of free will has been developed that:

1. Incorporates the strong points from both determinism and indeterminism.
2. Includes the notion of autonomy (though usually not called that by these philosophers).
3. Makes possible, if the process view is valid, a refutation of the views of Professors Flew and Mackie.
4. Has implications for a more radical notion of the limitations upon God's power than that confusedly introduced in the mainline tradition (see above pp. 41–44).
5. Seems both intuitively reasonable and consistent with what we have reason to believe we know about the way things work in the world.

The implications for this view of free will are all there in Whitehead's writings, but I shall rely on the work of Charles Hartshorne, who gives a more detailed and clearer explication of the relevant issues.[21] Again, in the interest of brevity and in order to avoid certain unfamiliar and unnecessary technicalities, I summarize his views.

According to Whitehead and Hartshorne, there is something akin to the free will of which humans are capable at all levels of nature. I say akin to, but they do not wish to imply identical with, or even extremely similar to. What Whitehead and Hartshorne do mean is best understood in the context of their description of the emergence of actual occasions. As mentioned above, the world is made up not of things, but of happenings, energy events, called by Whitehead, actual occasions. An actual occasion develops and that development takes some time (in the case of most of the events studied by, say, physics, a mere fraction of a second). The developing actual occasion includes a physical pole and a mental pole. The physical pole dominates in the early phase of the concrescence of the occasion, and is characterized chiefly by the shaping of the emerging occasion by causal efficacies transmitted from prior actual occasions. These causal efficacies determine the limits of what is possible for the emerging occasion, and in the case of many events at the purely physical level of reality (atomic energy reactions, simpler chemical reactions, etc.), the range of what is possible is extremely limited but not nonexistent. In speaking of a mental pole Whitehead and Hartshorne do not mean to imply consciousness. But they do insist that the emerging actual occasion, in the later phase of development and with some degree of responsiveness to the causal efficacies impinging upon it, is capable of further development in a novel and unpredictable way, not fully determined by the causal efficacies. In all natural events at every level is some degree of creativity, and the emergence of actualities that are new and not completely determined by or predictable from past events.

One interesting implication of this process view is a universalization of the concept of free will. To be sure, we have focused upon free will in the context of human actions, for that is where the entire focus has been placed in the traditional free will defense. But the actions of all entities and occasions exhibit, according to process philosophy, something akin to the free will and creativity found in much more developed ways among humans.

The physical pole, the causal efficacies that limit the possibilities open to the emerging actual occasion, must be kept in mind, especially when we consider the problem of natural evils, that is, evils not attributable to human misuse of free will. According to Whitehead, matter, or the physical world, is not, as in traditional Christian thought, created *de novo* and out of nothing by God. Matter is coeternal with God, and its causal efficacies set limits to what is possible even for God. God's lure of emerging events towards maximum satisfaction works within the limitations set by the physical reality with which God must work. The modern evolutionary view of the world indicates that newly emerging occasions are often not developments in the direction of maximal satisfaction. In the realm of biological evolution, novelties in emerging events are triggered by minute mutations in the genetic material; and the greater percentage of these mutations and their resulting novelties are deleterious, working against the maximization of satisfaction, and against the development of more complex, sensitive, and harmonious organism. Whitehead, and process thinkers generally, by no means deny this. The world of physical reality is not completely amenable to the lure of God's purpose. What we call natural evil, which is enormous in scope, is not to be accounted for by the will of God, or by human sin, but rather by random and often deleterious mutations within the chain of physical causal efficacies. In spite of all of this, however, Whitehead, and process thinkers generally, point out that even in the midst of all this entropy, there has in fact been a thrust towards the development of beings more and more sensitive to others, more and more capable of mutual harmony and cooperation, and closer to the beings who are capable of the kind of love that might culminate in the peaceable, loving, and just Kingdom of God.

There are limitations on what is possible, and yet there are creative options, novelties, something akin to free will, for all actual occasions in any cosmic context. These notions are intimately related to Whitehead's conception of God. He speaks of two aspects of the divine reality: the primordial nature of God and the consequent nature of God.[22] The primordial nature of God consists of all of the possibilities for development that inhere in the cosmic order. In contrast to the traditional notion of divine omnipotence, this enormous range of possibilities is not completely open to the will and purpose of God.

Two sorts of limitation upon God's power exist. (1) The possibilities for the future, even for God, are limited by what is possible, given the order of physical reality. (2) The physical pole, that is, the limitations imposed by the laws of nature, restrict what is possible even for God. This Whiteheadian view reminds one of the concept of God as the mind, or as the Stoics and the author of the Gospel of John called it, the "Logos."[23]

The consequent nature of God is that actual entity, which is somehow aware of, sensitive, and responsive to all past and present actual occasions as well as being, by virtue of the primordial nature, aware of the possibilities of the future. But the perfection of God's awareness is not thought of (as in classical theism) as including the specific realities of future occasions. This is because those realities of future occasions, though limited in possibilities by the causal efficacies that impinge upon them, are not fully determined, not even by God; for the future will include novelties that depend in part upon the way the developing mental pole of any actual occasion responds selectively and creatively to causal efficacies. The degree to which such creative freedom is possible for any given emerging actual occasion varies from the almost (but never absolutely) nonexistent to the very considerable degree existing in more complex and organic entities. God, as consequent nature, is aware of all actual occasions and possible interrelations. And it is the purpose and will of God to lure all occasions into the greatest possible harmony, the greatest possible organismic unity and, to use Whitehead's term, satisfaction. In Christian religious terms this is the divine thrust towards the Kingdom of God.

In *Process and Reality*, Whitehead calls his system speculative.[24] By this he does not mean it was spun out of sheer uncontrolled imagination, but rather many of its views, such as that just described in connection with the emergence of actual occasions, are hypothetical extrapolations from hard data (i.e. directly observable sense data). Nevertheless, Whitehead and his followers believe the notion of creative emergence, with some degree of freedom at all levels of nature, is a reasonable extrapolation from two sets of well established facts: namely the Heisenberg principle of uncertainty, and the fact of novelty in the process of evolution. According to Hartshorne, at the level of human conscious choice there is no need for extrapolation, for we have ample, direct, and irrefutable evidence of novelties that arise from such choices.

What I have just described is, incidentally, what Hartshorne means by indeterminism in the important article, "Freedom Requires Universal Causality and Indeterminism." Hartshorne does not mean or endorse the view articulated by some traditional philosophers and theologians, who have sought to refute the doctrine of determinism (or to refute Professors Flew and Mackie) by proposing an indeterminism, which implies that some events (e.g. those chosen with free will) are wholly independent of antecedent causes. Hartshorne's view may properly be called a third view, neither traditional determinism nor traditional indeterminism, but a view that incorporates the strong points of each. We might say that according to Hartshorne, acts of free will are partly determined and partly not determined.

Hartshorne's view seems intuitively sound when we consider the sort of events at the human level that are relevant to the concept of free will. Humans are connected to the rest of nature in all sorts of complex ways.

In connection with the choices they make with free will, those connections resemble a very sensitive and complex cybernetic system. To a very considerable extent, what the system is capable of at any given time is determined by the data that has been entered into it. When a new bit of data is entered, the system as a whole is to some degree reshaped by including the new data in all the ways it is relevant to all the other bits of data; new connections and new possibilities emerge.[25] There is a degree of freedom in how the cybernetic system will selectively respond to the given causal efficacies.

IMPLICATIONS

If the concept of free will that is found in process philosophy is correct, then the attacks made by Professors Flew and Mackie are refuted; for, as we recall, those attacks depended upon the doctrine of compatibilism—the view that there is no contradiction in saying of human free will choice that it is both completely determined and an act of free will. If the views of process philosophy are merely plausible, or only possibly true, then to that extent the attacks of Flew and Mackie are weakened.

The metaphysical system of process philosophy also includes, as the above descriptions imply, a view of the limitations upon God's power that is more radical than those that were, (rather grudgingly) admitted into mainline Christian tradition. All emerging actual occasions have, to a greater or lesser degree, the possibility of a novel and creative response to influences that impinge upon them, a response chosen by their own mental pole and not determined by anything else. The ideas of divine determinism are incompatible with this view. Thus, in process theology, God's power is the power of persuasion. God offers to each emerging actual occasion a range of possibilities ordered in such a way as to make most attractive the option that will lead to the greatest satisfaction. But alas, the choice of the best option is not forced, and the best option is often not chosen. Genuine autonomy is possible for all events, and is a necessary component of any action that is fully an act of free will.

From the perspective of process theology and ecological theology we could say there is indeed a God who is always and everywhere willing the mutual fulfillment of all things[26] in the Kingdom of God, but God is not omnipotent. God provides the lure towards the mutual fulfillment of all things, but his power is the power of persuasion, and the realization of the Kingdom of God in any full sense is partly dependent on us, and on the responses of all other actual occasions.

I want to mention two of the main criticisms that have been raised against the whole line of thought I have developed in this chapter. First, it is said that it is not only speculative but far too speculative. I have, at least at the present time, no knock down refutation of that criticism. I think process theology and ecological theology are indeed speculative and they are replete with questions and issues that require a great deal more in the way of inquiry and analysis. Nevertheless, these views, so far as I have been able to think them out, are logically coherent, and consistent with our best knowledge of the way things are in the world. Therefore and in this sense, reasonable. Second, another weighty objection is that God as conceived in process theology is far too weak. Sometimes this second objection is made by those bothered by the correct observation that the process views depart radically in some respects from traditional orthodoxy.

The most serious objection is that such a weak God cannot guarantee the fulfillment of his promises. In biblical literature, and in the writings of almost all of the theologians of the tradition, emphasis is placed on God's promise of the eventual realization of the Kingdom of God.[27] It is understood in the tradition that citizens of the Kingdom of God are only those whose characters are virtuous, capable of, and desiring, the life of love and justice. But if humans are so prone to or sunk in sin, or as indicated by Christian theologians, so lost in sin as to require God's powerful and gratuitous grace to have any hope of redemption, how can they of their free will attain the virtues required for citizenship in the Kingdom of God? The traditional answer is that they cannot. They are all unworthy and as St. Paul says slaves of sin.[28] They must be changed by a power that comes from beyond themselves and their corrupt wills: namely, by the grace of God. Only thus can we have complete confidence that the promises of God will be fulfilled.

But if, as indicated in process theology, God's power is such that he can only provide the lure towards virtue, can only seek to persuade, critics ask what hope is there that many, or indeed any, sinful humans will freely choose to love God and one another? Hope vanishes, the critics charge, or at the very least hope is greatly weakened.

There can be no doubt the process view of the limitations upon God's power entails a major and radical departure from the orthodox tradition and I indicate several reasons why we should welcome that departure:

1.   As indicated earlier, it is doubtful traditional free will defenders are successful in reconciling their doctrine of divine providence (essential to any guarantee that the promises of God will be fulfilled) with their

description of the way in which God freely limits his own power in order to make room for human free will in moral matters. This traditional scheme rules out the sort of genuine autonomy of humans that is necessary if one is to be able to withstand attacks such as that mounted by Professors Flew and Mackie (see chapter 3).

2. Descriptions of divine providence and omnipotence were traditionally coupled with the view (a) postadamic humans are so enslaved by sin they cannot not sin and (b) some are redeemed from that condition by the unmerited grace of God. Such a theological stance makes it impossible to give an acceptable answer to the question of why God does not give redeeming grace to all.

3. The traditional doctrines of divine providence and omnipotence, and the guarantee that by virtue of these the divine promises will be fulfilled, seems to me to imply that humans have no moral responsibility to make their contributions to the creation of a society in which love and justice reign.

4. The free will defense requires that humans have an autonomous free will,[29] that they cannot become fit for citizenship in the Kingdom of God unless they use that free will to choose to love God and one another. I have argued we should understand humans have the ability to learn to possess these qualities (see chapter 6). In any case, if humans posses such an autonomous free will, it is logically possible they will not choose to live by the requisite virtues. It is indeed logically possible that no humans will do so. And when we consider the state of the actual world, and the amount of hatred and strife in it, the belief there is a guarantee of the Kingdom of God seems rather like wishful thinking. One might argue that even in the world as it is with its over-supply of evil, there are nevertheless, by the grace of God, some virtuous saints, enough to supply some population for the Kingdom of God. But the vexing question arises: given the traditional notion of divine omnipotence, and the view that even virtuous saints have achieved their status only by virtue of the gratuitous grace of God, why could God not have done a better job of fulfilling his promises in greater abundance for a great many more humans, if indeed not for all?

AN ANALOGY FOR GOD'S RELATION TO CREATURES

Let us think in terms of the analogy frequently used in biblical literature: namely, that which likens God to a loving father, mindful that it is the love and not the gender of the lover which is to be stressed. With feminist insights and those of Bonhoeffer in mind this loving parent is responsible for discipline, judgment, and punishment, but concerned with these as instruments of his love. He is not to be thought of as the ruler of his children, or as the autocratic father/king, but as one who desires and consistently works for the growth of his children towards maturity and independence.

Let us think of this parent as the parent not of a family of a few children, living in a safe from the world house, but as the parent of countless billions and zillions of children, living in an unimaginable, perhaps infinite, realm of space and time; a father in touch with and concerned for the growth of all of his children to maturity and to satisfaction, a satisfaction, which consists (in very large part) of a mutual harmony of all of the children with each other. This is of course the implication of the process theology view.

Since the parent is a loving parent, concerned for the eventual independence of his children, his concern for this ultimate outcome is expressed not in the use of sheer force or autocratic command, but in the employment of education and persuasion. Again, the process view is evident.

Some Reservations and Modifications

There is much to be said for this analogy of God as a loving parent. It is attractive not only because it helps to solve some of the problems of theodicy, which cannot be solved if we adhere to traditionalist notions regarding God's relation to humans and to the world. It is attractive because it fits much better with a metaphysical view informed by knowledge of the way the world works that is far superior to older views.

There are, however, some problems with the way process thinkers have developed their theology and I should like to suggest some modifications.

The Darker Side of Reality

With considerable justice, process theology, as it deals with issues of theodicy, has been accused of being too rosy.[30] Robert C. Neville describes process theology as maintaining "that all evil puts unchangeable conditions on the future; but the future can make the best of those conditions and it has infinite resources for that task."[31] Process theology holds that God presents to each and every concrescing actual occasion (event in process of becoming) the entire range of possible outcomes in a graded order of value—that is, with outcomes that would lead to satisfaction made as appealing as possible. To be sure, the possible outcomes are limited by constraints from the causal efficacies from the past, but none of those absolutely determine the outcome. There is still plenty of room for growth and development in the direction of satisfaction. The critics to whom I refer suggest process thinkers have stressed, almost exclusively, the capacity of the persuasive God to bring about the best possible outcome. This criticism must be taken seriously. Such a rosy, optimistic conclusion is, in fact, unwarranted and inconsistent with the empirical data to which process thinkers pay homage. Human beings certainly have given more than ample evidence of their capacity for resisting the lure of the loving parent. If we are to cast our theology into the cosmic/ecological/evolutionary/ process modes, we might do well to understand the maladjustments and painful fatalities of the story of evolution in similar terms—as the failure to use whatever quantum of freedom the concrescing actual occasion has to respond to the lure towards satisfaction. Certainly there are spontaneous and unpredictable responses to given causal efficacies; but the story of evolution, and perhaps of human history, is that the majority of these are deleterious. The second law of thermodynamics suggests that in the long run, and overall, the process of nature and history is not towards satisfaction but towards death.

Does this mean that God is too weak to be a proper object of worship?[32] It does mean that God's power is limited to such an extent that he cannot guarantee the ultimate establishment of an eternal Kingdom of God, certainly not in this world. And undoubtedly for the majority of religious persons (certainly those of the mainline orthodox traditions), this means that the God of process thought is too weak, and, therefore, not truly God. One cannot even say that the process God has sufficient power to make such a happy outcome likely in the long run.

But what is the characteristic that makes God worthy of worship? The answer given by the process theologian is that God is always and everywhere working for the fullest possible satisfaction of all of his creatures. I must confess that, for me, that is quite sufficient. Our world exhibits far too much suffering, strife, hatred, and all manner of evils. But that is not the whole story. Even in the midst of these evils, there are many examples of the great good that comes from commitment to a God who is a loving parent. And even in the midst of the dis-teleologies of world evolution, are also teleological triumphs. Some power is and has been at work creating these goods. To the extent we can identify that power, even if we cannot fully understand it, that power deserves our worship.

GOD AND CREATION

Whitehead, and other process thinkers, attribute the limitations upon God's power to the fact that God is not the creator of matter or nature; matter/nature is just as eternal as God.[33] One might argue that this conclusion follows from the law of the conservation of mass/energy. But where did the conserved mass/energy come from? That is an ancient and impenetrable mystery.

Aspects of process thought, which are vital to the inquiry I have been pursuing, are quite independent of any particular theory about the ultimate origins of the world, or of anything else for that matter. To be sure, they are not independent of the traditionally orthodox view that God created the world out of nothing and controls all things absolutely. But there are many other theories that have been put forward. Given the fact that all of the relevant data comes to our finite minds from within the events of the already extant world, we have no way of knowing about the ultimate origins of the world itself.[34]

Though I have just commended a proper skepticism about ultimate origins, I might just mention that one way of reading the opening verses of Genesis appeals to me, and is in keeping with process thought. The most common English translation of Genesis 1:1–2 is: "In the beginning God created the heavens and the earth. The earth was without form and void ...". But in recent years, many scholars of the ancient Hebrew language have argued that a more accurate translation is: "When God began to create the heavens and the earth, the earth was without form and void. ..."[35]

The alternative reading strongly suggests and is certainly compatible with the view that God's initial creative work was performed upon an already existent, though formless, matter. Scholars of ancient Near Eastern religions suggest that the Hebrew for formless and void (vohu and tohu) is equivalent to the chaos (Tiamat) of ancient Babylonian cosmology. In the Babylonian version of creation, Marduk created the world as we know it by defeating Tiamat and creating a formed, ordered world out of it. The practice of relying upon parallels with Babylonian texts is supported by the fact that there are many passages in the Hebrew text, which very closely resemble older Babylonian texts. One of the best known instances of this is the Hebrew flood story, which is extremely similar to the flood passages in the Babylonian "Gilgamesh Epic."[36]

Traditional Christian and Jewish ways of reading the creation text reflects a theological dogma that slowly emerged chiefly through the work of the great literary prophets of the Hebrew Bible. That dogma is precisely the doctrine of the absolute omnipotence of God. This doctrine is but-tressed and perhaps logically implied by the companion doctrine that God created the world out of nothing (ex nihilo). The ex nihilo doctrine is incompatible with the alternative (Babylonian-type) translation of Genesis 1:1–2, but it is worth noting it is an absolutely mind-boggling mystery (see chapter 8, note 34).

My conclusion, or bias, is that both the Whiteheadian process view and the traditional view lie in the realm of the unknowable. True, the Whiteheadian view, for which I indicate a preference, implies God does not rule over anything with absolute power. All actual occasions have some power of their own, and some degree, however small in most instances, of self direction with regard to the possibilities open to them. And, at the human level, if all power whatsoever is directed by God alone, then, as Calvin deduced, whether we do or do not accept the grace of God (the lure of God towards satisfaction, in Whiteheadian terms) is wholly dictated by God. Just as those who are reprobate cannot not sin, those who receive God's grace receive a grace which is, as Calvin said, irresistible.[37]

Still, on the issue of the ultimate origins of things, and of the ultimate causes of our choices, I find myself in darkness and ignorance. We can see the unacceptable implications of the strict omnipotence tradition, but the reality of these ultimates is beyond our knowledge. I would add, however, the traditional strict omnipotence line not only has unacceptable implica-tions, but is, theologically dispensable; not only dispensable, but dispensa-ble with good riddance. For it tends to rob humans of responsibility, of any real sense that they have a vital role to play in the realization of the king-dom of peace and justice. Furthermore, if we are to allow empirical evi-dence to shape our judgments, as we certainly should, we have ample reason to believe that God's will, presumably at work in all things, is often resisted. Just as dis-teleology is writ large in the process of evolution, so it is found disturbingly present in human affairs.

In conclusion, I urge, in response to criticism the God of process theo-logy is too weak, that the process view does not at all imply God is nearly as weak as these critics suggest. The divine grace is at work always and everywhere, presenting to emerging actual occasions possibilities for their future. The presentation is, however, in an order weighted in favor of those possibilities that lead to the greatest satisfaction. It always seeks to persuade the emerging actual occasion into a more inclusive society characterized by wider and deeper mutual sensitivity and support. At the human level, we know that the prospect of such a venture, into new and unknown situa-tions, into relationships that often asks us to curb our self-interests for the welfare of others, can seem frightening. And we know that all too often people, out of self-interest or fear, refuse to make that venture. Yet, the satisfactions for those who make the venture are very real, and highly conducive to great joy, which comes only with the experience of mutual love. If the power of God, like all of his attributes, is perfect, then perhaps we should think of it in the following way: God has all the power that any being could possibly have, in a cosmos where individuals who possess, to varying degrees, free will and, therefore, as implied in the concept of free will, some power of their own.

Process theology suggests the venture of which I have spoken is not for humans alone. It asks us to see the cosmos in a new way in which all of the creations of God are (even if unaware of it) intimately related to one another; and if they are aware of it and are willing to give it expression in their lives, intimately related to one another in a society of love and justice.

Notes

CHAPTER 1   INTRODUCTION

1.   Epicurus, "On the Anger of God," trans. W. Fletcher, in *Ante-Nicene Fathers: The Writings of the Fathers Down to A.D. 325*, ed. Alexander Roberts and James Donaldson, vol. 7 (Grand Rapids, Mich.: Eerdmans, 1951), chap. 13.

2.   G. W. F. Leibniz, *Theodicy: Essays on the Goodness of God, the Freedom of Man and the Origin of Evil*, trans. E. M. Huggard (London: Routledge, 1952).

3.   As we shall see the Eastern Orthodox tradition differs in significant ways from the western version of the free will defense.

4.   *Romans* 9:20 has been regarded by many an enemy of theodicy as a decisive proof text.

5.   See John E. Thiel, *Nonfoundationalism* (Minneapolis, Minn.: Fortress, 1994).

6.   See F. Berthold, "Logical Empiricism and Philosophical Theology," *Journal of Religion* 25 (1955): 207–17.

CHAPTER 2   THE CENTRAL IMPORTANCE OF THE FREE WILL DEFENSE

1.   The Christian Science tradition really is no exception in my opinion. While it denies the reality of evil, its reasoning on this point is derived basically from the Vedanta philosophy of Hinduism.

2.   See *I John* 4:7–12.

3.   Augustine, *The City of God*, trans. M. Dods (New York: Modern Library, 1950), bk. 11, chaps. 11 and 13.

4.   Augustine, *City*, bk. 11, chap. 18.

5.   Augustine, "De Genesi: Imperfectus Liber," in *Patrologia Cursus Completus*, ed. J.-P. Migne, n.p., n.d., 34:222. "*Malo vera non esse naturalia; sed omne quod dicitur malum, aut peccatum esse, aut poenam peccati.*"

6.   Augustine, *City*, bk. 14, chap. 11.

7. Augustine, *City*, bk. 11, chap. 18.

8. Augustine, "The Free Choice of the Will," in *The Teacher, The Free Choice of the Will, Grace and Free Will*, trans. R. P. Russell (Washington, D.C.: Catholic University of America Press, 1968), bk. 3, chap. 19, sect. 26.

9. See, for example, N. Smart, "Omnipotence, Evil and Supermen," in *God and Evil*, ed. N. Pike (Englewood Cliffs, N.J.: Prentice Hall, 1964), 106, where he suggests that for humans to be rebuilt so as to be perfectly good, with no hint of evil, "would mean that the ascription of goodness would become unintelligible. ... Moral utterance is embedded in the cosmic status quo." In Smart's defense, however, one should note that these remarks are made with reference to what he calls a cosmomorphic universe—a universe as ours actually is. He does not deny that God could have made a different sort.

10. *John* 3:16; and *I John* 4:7–12.

11. I refer to this theme a number of times as the "*O Felix Culpa*" theme. See the Roman Catholic Missal, the "*Exultet*" passage read on Easter Eve. The Latin text reads, "*O certe necessarium Adae peccatum, quod Christi morte deletum est! O felix culpa, quae talem ac tantum meruit habere redemptorem!*"

12. *Ephesians* 6:12–13.

13. S. Kierkegaard, *The Concept of Anxiety*, ed. R. Thomte (Princeton: Princeton University Press, 1980), 25–30.

14. Kierkegaard, *Concept*, 29.

15. Kierkegaard, *Concept*, 44.

CHAPTER 3   WHY DOESN'T GOD CAUSE US TO HAVE A WHOLLY VIRTUOUS FREE WILL?

1. J. L. Mackie, "Evil and Omnipotence," *Mind* 64 (April 1955): 200–12; and A. Flew, "Divine Omnipotence and Human Freedom," in *New Essays in Philosophical Theology*, ed. A. Flew and A. Macintyre (London: SCM Press, 1955.) Though the criticism which follows has been discussed by many in subsequent years, the two articles I refer to, in my opinion, focus more forcefully, clearly and succinctly upon the precise point at which the traditional free will defense is vulnerable. These articles also implicitly raise the point, which I shall discuss below, that discussions of these issues have in general suffered from the lack of a clear and adequate concept of free will.

2. According to the traditional argument, this includes also natural evils, for those arose as punishments for sin and would not exist had not humans used their free will to rebel against God. It is customary amongst philosophers to call all of those evils which arise through human wickedness as moral evils and all other evils (e.g. suffering due to arthritis) as natural evils. The traditional argument in a sense collapses all evils into moral evils.

3. Mackie says "no limits" to what God can do, but in the mainline tradition it was agreed that there is one limit: namely, even God cannot do anything which involves a logical contradiction. Indeed, Mackie's own argument makes it clear that he has this limit in mind.

4. Mackie, 200.

5. Mackie, 209.

6. Flew, 149.

7. Flew, 149.

8. Flew, 150.

9. Flew, 151.

10. B. F. Skinner, *Science and Human Behavior* (New York: Macmillan, 1953). Flew does not, however, refer to Skinner.

11. A. Plantinga, *God, Freedom and Evil* (New York: Harper Torchbooks, 1974), 30.

12. Plantinga, 29.

13. J. Calvin, *Institutes of the Christian Religion*, ed. J. T. McNeill (Philadelphia: Westminster, 1960), bk. 1, chap. 16, sect. 4.

14. Calvin, *Institutes*, bk. 2, chap. 3, sect. 5; and bk. 2, chap. 4, sect. 1 (emphasis added).

15. Calvin, *Institutes*, bk. 1, chap. 16, sect. 8.

16. Calvin, *Institutes*, bk. 1, chap. 16, sect. 8.

17. J. Calvin, *Concerning the Eternal Predestination of God* (London: James Clarke, 1961), 179.

18. Calvin, *Predestination*, 181.

19. Calvin, *Institutes*, bk. 1, chap. 15, sect. 8. Here Calvin asserts that God could have made man so that he "either could not or would not sin at all." He then condemns as iniquitous the question as to why God did not so create humans.

20. Calvin, *Institutes*, bk. 1, chap. 15, sect. 8.

21. Calvin, *Institutes*, bk. 1, chap. 15, sect. 1.

22. Calvin, *Institutes*, bk. 2, chap. 3, sect. 5.

23. Calvin, *Institutes*, bk. 2, chap. 3, sect. 5.

24. *Romans* 6:17.

25. Calvin, *Institutes*, bk. 3, chap. 23, sect. 5.

26. Calvin, *Institutes*, bk. 3, chap. 23, sect. 7.

27. Thomas Aquinas, *Summa Theologica*, trans. by the Fathers of the English Dominican Province (Allen, Tex.: Christian Classics, Thomas More Publishing Co.), 1:110, pt. 1, quest. 19, art. 8.

28. Aquinas, *Summa Theologica*. See *both* 1:110, pt. 1, quest. 19, art. 8 *and* 1:418, pt. 1, quest. 83, art. 1.

29. Aquinas, *Summa Theologica*, 2:967, pt. 1–2, quest. 85, art. 2.

30. S. Kierkegaard, *The Sickness unto Death*, ed. and trans. H. V. and E. H. Hong (Princeton: Princeton University Press, 1980).

31. S. Kierkegaard, *Kierkegaard's Concluding Unscientific Postscript*, trans. D. F. Swenson and W. Lowrie (Princeton: Princeton University Press, 1941), 115 ff.

32.   Kierkegaard, *Postscript*, 232. The same idea is expressed in *The Sickness unto Death*, where he speaks of God as having made humans as a relationship which relates itself to itself. He says "that God who made man a relationship lets this go as it were out of his hand." *Sickness*, 149.

33.   S. Kierkegaard, *Philosophical Fragments*, trans. D. F. Swenson (Princeton: Princeton University Press, 1936), 19–21.

34.   S. Kierkegaard, *Training in Christianity*, trans. W. Lowrie (Princeton: Princeton University Press, 1947), 159–60. This passage reminds one of the point made in Kierkegaard's discourse of the Expectation of Faith, where he stresses that no one can give faith to another, but faith must be freely chose for oneself. See "The Expectation of Faith," in *Edifying Discourses*, ed. P. Holmer, trans. D. F. and L. M. Swenson (New York: Harper Torchbooks, 1958).

35.   Irenaeus, "Irenaeus Against Heresies," in *Ante-Nicene Fathers*, 1:518.

36.   Irenaeus, 521.

37.   Irenaeus, 522–23 (emphasis added).

CHAPTER 4   SHOULD THE TRADITIONAL FREE WILL DEFENSE BE REVISED?

1.   *II Corinthians* 5:19.

2.   Universalism seems to be implied by *Colossians* 1:15–20.

3.   See, for example, Anselm, *Proslogioum, Monologium, An Appendix in Behalf of the Fool by Gaunilon, and Cur Deus Homo*, trans. S. N. Deane (Chicago: Open Court, 1945), 13–14. See also the denial by Thomas Aquinas that relations in the world are real in God, *Summa Theologica*, 1:119 and 151–2, pt. 1, quest. 21, art. 3, and pt. 1, quest. 28, art. 1 respectively.

4.   A persuasive description of the pathos of God may be found in A. J. Heschel, *The Prophets* (New York: Jewish Publication Society of America, 1962).

5.   In the Roman Catholic tradition the preeminence of Thomas Aquinas's theology is still evident. See the Encyclical letter of Pope Leo XIII, "On the Restoration of Christian Philosophy according to the Mind of St. Thomas Aquinas, the Angelic Doctor," August 4, 1879, reprinted in vol. 1 of the 1948 edition of the *Summa Theologica*.

6.   It is still worth while to read H. E. Fosdick, *A Guide to Understanding the Bible* (New York: Harper, 1938). Even if one is skeptical of the evolutionary slant in this work, Fosdick sets forth in abundance the specific texts which exhibit significant variations and changes in basic theological concepts, including the concept of God.

7.   *Exodus* 15:3.

8.   *Joshua* 10:13–14.

9.   *I Samuel* 15:1–3.

10.   *I Samuel* 15:9.

11.   *I Samuel* 16.

12. *Exodus* 23:22.

13. *Isaiah* 10:5–6.

14. *Amos* 9:7.

15. See "The Church," in *The Documents of Vatican II*, ed. W. M. Abbott and J. Gallagher (New York: The America Press, 1966), para. 16, 34–5.

CHAPTER 5   THE CONCEPT OF A LIMITED GOD

1. P. Melanchthon, *Melanchthon on Christian Doctrine*, trans. Clyde L. Manschreck (Grand Rapids, Mich.: Baker Book House, 1982). See especially chaps. 5 and 6.

2. Thomas Aquinas, *Summa Theologica*, bk. 1, 107, pt. 1, quest. 19, sect. 6.

3. Thomas Aquinas, *Summa Theologica*, sect. 7, 109.

4. Thomas Aquinas, *Summa Theologica*, sect. 3, 105.

5. Thomas Aquinas, *Summa Theologica*, sect. 12, 113.

6. Thomas Aquinas, *Summa Theologica*, quest. 22, sect. 2, 123.

7. Thomas Aquinas, *Summa Theologica*, quest. 83, sect. 1, 418. Thomas also in this connection quotes with approval the passage from *Ecclesiaticus* 15:14, "God made man from the beginning and left him in the hand of his own counsel."

8. St. Thomas Aquinas, *Summa Theologica*, vol. 4, 1864, pts. 2a–2ae, quest. 165, sect. 1. This passage clearly indicates that, according to St. Thomas, Adam was created with free will de novo. Thomas also adds with approval the statement of Augustine,

> It seems to me that man would have no prospect of any special praise if he were able to lead a good life simply because there was none to persuade him to lead an evil life, since both by nature he had the power and in his power he had the will, not to consent to the persuader.

See Augustine, *The Literal Meaning of Genesis*, trans. J. H. Taylor (New York, Newman, 1982), 2:137. The Taylor translation differs from St. Thomas Aquinas with regard to some specific words, but not at all in meaning.

9. Thomas Aquinas, *Summa Theologica*, 1:108, pt. 1, quest. 19, sect. 6.

10. Thomas Aquinas, *Summa Theologica*, 2:636, pt. 1–2, quest. 10, sect. 4.

11. Thomas Aquinas, *On the Truth of the Catholic Faith: Summa Contra Gentiles*, trans. A. C. Pegis (Garden City: Image Books, 1955), bk. 1, 266.

12. Thomas Aquinas, *Summa Contra Gentiles*, 1:266.

13. Thomas Aquinas, *Summa Contra Gentiles*. This sort of distinction aroused the ire, sarcasm and denunciation of Martin Luther, who, as the following quote demonstrates, preceded Calvin in asserting a divine determinism:

> Do you suppose that He does not will what He foreknows, or that He does not foreknow what He wills? If He wills what he foreknows, His

will is eternal and changeless, because His nature is so. From which it follows, by resistless logic, that all we do, however it may appear to us to be done mutably and contingently, is in reality done necessarily and immutably in respect of God's will. ... Since then His will is not impeded, what is done cannot but be done where, when, how, as far as and by whom He foresees and wills. (*Martin Luther: Selections from His Writings,* ed. J. Dillenberger [Garden City, N.Y.: Anchor, 1961], 181.)

14.   *New Catholic Encyclopedia* (New York: McGraw-Hill Book Co., 1967), 6:90.

CHAPTER 6   THE CONCEPT OF FREE WILL

1.   See T. Duggan and B. Gert, "Free Will as the Ability to Will," *Nous* 13 (1979): 197–217.

2.   The concept of an autonomous will is more fully developed in chapter 8, p. **000**.

3.   Augustine, "On Two Souls: Against the Manichaens," in *A Select Library of the Nicene and Post-Nicene Fathers of the Christian Church,* ed. P. Schaff, vol. 4 (New York: Christian Literature Co., 1887), pt. 10, sect. 14.

4.   The analysis which follows is much indebted to the work of Professors Duggan and Gert, cited above. I have, however, somewhat adapted their analysis in order to stress the notion of free will as the ability to exercise rational control over one's desires and volitions, a notion clearly implicit in their work. And I have added the category of autonomous to the conditions they specify, a category not necessary for the concept of free will generally, but necessary for the sort of free will that is required for a more adequate free will defense in theodicy.

5.   Duggan and Gert, 202–203.

6.   I say may provide him with an excuse, because there are cases in which one is properly held to be morally responsible, even in the absence of explicit intention, as for example when one is negligent.

7.   H. Frankfort, "Freedom of the Will and the Concept of a Person," *Journal of Philosophy* 68/1 (January 1971): 5–20.

8.   Frankfort, 8.

9.   Frankfort, 7. I myself would suggest that there is increasing evidence that there is no absolute and sharp difference between the human and the animal world. The capacity of chimpanzees, for example, to invent new behavioral responses and useful tools, suggests to me at least some capacity for reflective self-evaluation.

10.   Frankfort, 10–14.

11.   Frankfort, 15.

12.   Frankfort, 7.

13.   Frankfort, 16.

14.   Frankfort, 16.

15. Frankfort, 16.

16. Frankfort, 19.

17. Frankfort, 7.

18. Aristotle, "Nichomachean Ethics," in *The Basic Works of Aristotle*, ed. R. McKeon, vol. 3 (New York: Random House, 1941), chap. 1.

19. Aristotle, "Nichomachean Ethics," vol. 3, chap. 1.

20. Duggan and Gert, 209–10.

21. Following the somewhat awkward terminology of Duggan and Gert, I use the term unvoluntary rather than involuntary, because the latter is often used to refer to reflex actions.

22. Augustine, *De libero arbitrio: libre tres = The Free Choice of the Will: Three Books*, Latin text and English translation by F. E. Tourscher (Philadelphia: Peter Reilly, 1937), bk. 3, chap. 8.

23. Augustine, *De libero arbitrio*, bk. 3, chap. 7.

24. These notions, developed by Culver and Gert, are crucial to the understanding of certain types of mental disorders. It is interesting that the third edition (1980) of the American Psychiatric Association's definitive *Diagnostic and Statistical Manual of Mental Disorder* has revised earlier definitions to take account of these concepts. See C. M. Culver and B. Gert, *Philosophy in Medicine* (New York: Oxford University Press, 1982), chap. 5.

25. Frankfort, 19.

26. Frankfort, 19.

27. Frankfort, 20.

28. Frankfort, 20.

29. Plantinga, 29.

CHAPTER 7   A REVISED FREE WILL DEFENSE

1. I use the term creatures rather than humans, because in my final chapter I want to suggest that God intends that all things should be included in the Kingdom of God.

2. I am aware that most traditional theologians have held that divine love existed from eternity, even before the creation of the world, and that it is the love shared among the persons of the trinity. They have, however, also maintained that this divine love is overflowing and is the ultimate reason for the creation of the world, and the goal is that this love be shared amongst all humans, for that would be the completion of the creation of humans in the image of God.

3. It is suffering pain when there is no good reason for it, or good consequence expected from it, in other words pain for its own sake. Thus, the pain inflicted by a benevolent dentist, while not pleasant, is a good instrumental to the repair of a damaged tooth. And, if one should argue that pain is not evil for the masochist, I would point out that that is because he or she gets pleasure from it.

4. Origen, *On First Principles*, trans. G. W. Butterworth (New York: Harper Torchbooks, 1966), 130.

5.   John Hick, *Evil and the God of Love* (San Francisco: Harper and Row, 1966), 253 ff.

6.   That there is in fact a single and clearly defined Christian tradition is, I think, open to serious question. My citations of changes and contrasting, and even contradictory, views in chapters 4 and 5 support this skepticism. I have, however, tried to focus with regard to the free will defense upon the extremely influential and widely shared views of Augustine.

CHAPTER 8   AN ECOLOGICAL THEOLOGY

1.   I mention only one widely read example: Edgar Brightman, *The Problem of God* (Nashville: Abingdon, 1940).

2.   A work of great value in this connection is: Charles Birch and John Cobb, *The Liberation of Life* (Cambridge: Cambridge University Press, 1981).

3.   *Genesis* 1:31.

4.   *Isaiah* 65:25.

5.   *Isaiah* 55:12.

6.   *John* 1:1–3.

7.   *Romans* 8:22–23.

8.   *Colossians* 1:15–17.

9.   *2 Corinthians* 5:19.

10.   See Charles Hartshorne, *The Logic of Perfection* (Lasalle, Ill: Open Court, 1962).

11.   *Romans* 9:18 Paul is referring to *Exodus*: chaps. 7–10.

12.   *Romans* 9:18–20.

13.   Calvin, *Predestination* 88; also 84–88.

14.   Nancy Frankenberry, "Classical Theism, Pantheism and Pantheism: On the Relation between God and Gender Construction," *Zygon* 28/1 (March 1993): 32.

15.   It is the loving rather than the gender of the parent which is relevant, as feminist theologians insist.

16.   D. Bonhoeffer, *Letters and Papers from Prison* (London: SCM Press, Fontana Books, 1953). See especially the entries for April 30 and June 8, 1944.

17.   See Birch and Cobb.

18.   A. N. Whitehead, *Process and Reality* (New York: Macmillan, 1929).

19.   See David R. Griffin, *God, Power and Evil: A Process Theodicy* (Philadelphia: Westminster, 1976) and *Evil Revisited: Responses and Reconsideration* (Albany: State University of New York Press, 1981).

20.   W. Whitman, "Song of Myself" (excerpt), in *The Complete Poems*, ed. F. Murphy (London: Penguin, 1996), 115–16.

21.   See "Freedom Requires Universal Causality and Indeterminism," in Hartshorne, 161–90.

22. Whitehead, 521–6.

23. *John* 1:1.

24. Whitehead, 7–8.

25. The cybernetic, or computer, model is misleading in one very important respect. The feedback mechanisms are limited by the hard wiring of the computer itself. Recent brain research has indicated that, when a certain neuron fires, there are tens of millions of possible ways in which it may be integrated into the total brain system, modifying and being modified by the brain as a whole. See Gerald M. Edelman and Giulio Tonini, *A Universe of Consciousness: How Matter Becomes Imagination* (New York: Basic Books, 2000).

26. Again I refer to *Colossians* 1:19–20.

27. *Romans* 3:23–24 and 5:6.

28. *Romans* 6:16–17.

29. Insistence upon an autonomous will appear very early in the Christian tradition. See, for example, Origen, 77. There he writes: "It is for this reason, we think, that God, the parent of all things, in providing for *the salvation of his entire creation* through the unspeakable plan of his word and wisdom, has so ordered everything that each spirit or soul … should not be compelled by force against its free choice to any action *except that to which the motions of its own mind leads it*" (emphasis added).

30. See, for example, Nancy Frankenberry, "Some Problems in Process Theology," *Religious Studies* 17 (June 1981): 179–97.

31. R. Neville, *Creativity and God: A Challenge to Process Theology* (New York: Seabury, 1980), 69.

32. S. L. Ely, *The Religious Availability of Whitehead's God* (Madison: University of Wisconsin Press, 1942).

33. Whitehead, 524–33.

34. In his *Critique of Pure Reason*, in the section "The Antinomy of Pure Reason: First Conflict of the Transcendental Ideas" (trans. John Watson [Glasgow: James Maclehose & Sons, 1888], 158–60), Immanuel Kant offers opposing and contradictory proofs (a) "that the world has a beginning in time and is enclosed within limits of space," and (b) "that the world has no beginning in time and no limits in space, but is infinite as regards both time and space." If one assumes that the world has no beginning in time, then the world is preceded by an infinity of time, but no infinite series can be completed as a finite point of time; an infinite time cannot lead to a beginning of a world which includes finite moments of time. But if we assume, on the other hand, that the world had a beginning in time, then that which preceded that time was an empty time, a time which included nothing which could be a condition for existence. In common sense language: if the world had a beginning in time, what came before it that caused it to be?; and if it had no beginning in time, what caused that eternal world to exist, for nothing exists without a cause.

35. This alternative is indicated in a footnote to *Genesis* 1:1 in recent editions of the *Oxford Annotated Bible* (New York: Oxford University Press, 1962).

36. *Enuma Elish: The Seven Tablets of Creation*, ed. L. W. King (London: Luzac, 1902), 1:3. E. A. Speiser gives the following translation of *Genesis* 1:1–2: "When God set

about to create heaven and earth, the world being then a formless waste, with darkness over the seas and only an awesome wind sweeping over the water…" (*The Anchor Bible: Genesis*, trans. E. A. Speiser [Garden City, New York: Doubleday, 1964], 3).

37.   That for Calvin divine grace is irresistible is clearly implied by the passage in his *Institutes of the Christian Religion*, bk. 2, chap. 3, sect. 7.

Bibliography

Abbott, Walter M., ed. *The Documents of Vatican II*. New York: Guild Press, 1966.

American Psychiatric Association. *Diagnostic and Statistical Manual of Mental Disorders (DSM-III)*. Washington, D.C.: American Psychiatric Publishing, 1980.

The Anchor Bible: Genesis. Translated by Ephraim A. Speiser. Garden City, N.Y.: Doubleday, 1964.

Anselm. *Proslogium, Monologium, An Appendix in Behalf of the Fool and Cur Deus Homo*. Translated by Sidney N. Deane. Chicago: Open Court Publishing Co., 1945.

Aquinas, Thomas. *On the Truth of the Catholic Faith: Summa Contra Gentiles*. Book 1. Translated by A.C. Pegis. Garden City, N.Y.: Image Books, 1955.

————. *Summa Theologica*. Translated by the Fathers of the English Dominican Province. Vol. 4. Allen, Tex.: Christian Classics, Thomas More Publishing Co., 1981.

Aristotle. *The Basic Works of Aristotle*. Edited by Richard McKeon. New York: Random House, 1941.

Augustine. *The City of God*. Translated by Marcus Dods. New York: Modern Library, 1950.

————. "De Genesi: Imperfectus Liber." In *Patrologia Cursus Completus*, ed. J. P. Migne. Vol. 34. N.p. N.d.

————. *De libero arbitrio: libre tres* (The free choice of the will: Three books). Latin text and English translation by F.E. Tourscher. Philadelphia: Peter Reilly, 1937.

————. *The Literal Meaning of Genesis*. Translated by John H. Taylor. New York: Newman Press, 1982.

————. "On Two Souls: Against the Manichaeans." In *A Select Library of the Nicene and Post-Nicene Fathers of the Christian Church*, edited by Philip Schaff. Vol. 4. New York: The Christian Literature Co., 1887.

————. *Saint Augustine: The Teacher, The Free Choice of the Will, Grace and Free Will*. Translated by Robert P. Russell. Washington, D.C.: Catholic University of America Press, 1968.

Berthold, Fred, Jr. "Logical Empiricism and Philosophical Theology." *Journal of Religion* 25 (1955): 207–17.

Birch, Charles, and John B. Cobb. *The Liberation of Life*. Cambridge: Cambridge University Press, 1981.

Bonhoeffer, Dietrich. *Letters and Papers from Prison*. London: SCM Press, Fontana Books, 1953.

Brightman, Edgar S. *The Problem of God*. Nashville, Tenn.: Abingdon Press, 1940.

Calvin, John. *Concerning the Eternal Predestination of God*. London: James Clarke & Co., 1961.

————. *Institutes of the Christian Religion*. Edited by J. T. McNeill. Philadelphia: Westminster Press, 1960.

Culver, Charles M., and Bernard Gert. *Philosophy in Medicine*. New York: Oxford University Press, 1982.

Duggan, Timothy, and Bernard Gert. "Free Will as the Ability to Will." *Nous* 13 (1979): 197–217.

Edelman, Gerald M., and Giulio Tonini. *A Universe of Consciousness: How Matter Becomes Imagination*. New York: Basic Books, 2000.

Ely, S. L. *The Religious Availability of Whitehead's God*. Madison: University of Wisconsin Press, 1942.

Flew, Antony, and Alasdair Macintyre, eds. *New Essays in Philosophical Theology*. London: SCM Press, 1955.

Fosdick, Harry Emerson. *A Guide to Understanding the Bible*. New York: Harper and Brothers, 1938.

Frankenberry, Nancy. "Christian Theism, Pantheism and Panentheism: On the Relation Between God and Gender Construction." *Zygon* 28/1 (March 1993).

————. "Some Problems in Process Theology." *Religious Studies* 17 (June 1981): 179–97.

Frankfort, H. "Freedom of the Will and the Concept of a Person." *Journal of Philosophy* 68/1 (January 1971): 5–20.

Griffin, David R. *Evil Revisited: Responses and Reconsideration*. Albany: State University of New York Press, 1981.

Hartshorne, Charles. *The Divine Relativity: A Social Conception of God*. New Haven, Conn.: Yale University Press, 1964.

————. *The Logic of Perfection*. Lasalle, Ill.: Open Court Publishing Co., 1962.

Heschel, Abraham J. *The Prophets*. New York: Jewish Publication Society of America, 1962.

Hick, John. *Evil and the God of Love*. New York: Harper and Row, 1987.

Kane, Robert, and Stephen H. Phillips, eds. *Hartshorne, Process Philosophy, and Theology*. Albany: State University of New York Press, 1989.

Kant, Immanuel. *The Critique of Pure Reason*. Translated by John Watson. Glasgow: James Maclehose & Sons, 1888.

Kierkegaard, Soren. *The Concept of Anxiety.* Edited by Reidar Thomte. Princeton N.J.: Princeton University Press, 1980.

————. *Edifying Discourses: A Selection.* Edited by Paul Holmer, translated by David F. Swenson and Lillian M. Swenson. New York: Harper Torchbooks, 1958.

————. *Kierkegaard's Concluding Unscientific Postscript.* Translated by David F. Swenson and Walter Lowrie. Princeton, N.J.: Princeton University Press, 1941.

————. *Philosophical Fragments; Or, a Fragment of Philosophy.* Translated by David F. Swenson. Princeton, N.J.: Princeton University Press, 1936.

————. *The Sickness Unto Death.* Edited and translated by Howard V. Hong and Edna H. Hong. Princeton N.J.: Princeton University Press, 1980.

————. *Training in Christianity.* Translated by Walter Lowrie. Princeton: Princeton University Press, 1947.

King, Leonard W., ed. *Enuma Elish: The Seven Tablets of Creation.* London: Luzac and Co., 1902.

Leibniz, Gottfried Wilhelm. *Theodicy: Essays on the Goodness of God, the Freedom of Man and the Origin of Evil.* Translated by E.M. Huggard. London: Routledge and Kegan Paul, 1952.

Luther, Martin. *Martin Luther: Selections from His Writings.* Edited by John Dillenberger. Garden City, N.Y.: Anchor Books, 1961.

Mackie, John L. "Evil and Omnipotence." *Mind* 64 (April 1955): 200–12.

Melanchthon, Philip. *Melanchthon on Christian Doctrine.* Translated by Clyde L. Manschreck. Grand Rapids, Mich.: Baker Book House, 1982.

Neville, Robert C. *Creativity and God: A Challenge to Process Theology.* New York: Seabury Press, 1980.

Origen. *On First Principles.* Translated by George W. Butterworth. New York: Harper Torchbooks, 1966.

Oxford Annotated Bible. New York: Oxford University Press, 1962.

Pike, Nelson, ed. *God and Evil: Readings on the Theological Problem of Evil.* Englewood Cliffs, N.J.: Prentice Hall, 1964.

Plantinga, Alvin. *God, Freedom and Evil.* New York: Harper Torchbooks, 1974.

Roberts, Alexander and James Donaldson, eds. *Ante-Nicene Fathers: The Writings of the Fathers Down to A.D.* 325. Vol. 7. Grand Rapids, Mich.: Eerdmans, 1951.

Skinner, B. F. *Science and Human Behavior.* New York: Macmillan, 1953.

Thiel, John E. *Nonfoundationalism.* Minneapolis, Minn.: Fortress Press, 1994.

Whitehead, Alfred North. *Process and Reality.* New York: Macmillan, 1929.

Whitman, Walt. *Leaves of Grass.* Boston: Thayer and Eldridge, 1860–61.

Index of Names

Index of Subjects